EMBRACING
THE PROPHETIC

EMBRACING
THE PROPHETIC

By

Eileen Fisher

Destiny Image® Publishers, Inc.
P.O. Box 310
Shippensburg, PA 17257-0310

"Speaking to the Purposes of God for this Generation and for the Generations to Come."

For Worldwide Distribution, Printed in the U.S.A.

ISBN 10: 0-7684-2407-0

ISBN 13: 978-0-7684-2407-2

This book and all other Destiny Image, Revival Press, MercyPlace, Fresh Bread, Destiny Image Fiction, and Treasure House books are available at Christian bookstores and distributors worldwide.

For a U.S. bookstore nearest you, call
1-800-722-6774.

For more information on foreign distributors, call
717-532-3040.

Or reach us on the Internet:
www.destinyimage.com

1 2 3 4 5 6 7 8 9 10 11 / 09 08 07 06

Dedication

To the Body of Christ and all those who earnestly desire to prophesy and clearly hear the voice of God's Spirit.

To my wonderful family:

My husband, Fred—I can't imagine not sharing my life with you. Truly you are a gift from God.

My parents, Bernard and Ruth Flanagan, who loved me well.

My brothers: Bob, Jerry, David, Tim, and Willy; and my sisters: Rosemary, Ruthie, Lenore, and Liz. You made our one-bedroom house feel huge with all the fun and laughter.

My son, Michael, who is waiting for me in Heaven.

My daughter, Theresa, who has made my life worth living. You are my champion.

My steadfast son-in-law, Michael.

My daughter-in-law, Cindy, who gave me my wonderful grandsons Chris and Richard. They are priceless to me.

My grandson Garrett, who owns my heart; and my granddaughter, Gabrielle, who is a jewel in my crown.

I love, treasure, and cherish you all.

Acknowledgments

I would like to give all the glory, praise, and honor to the Father, Son, and Holy Spirit. For They have commissioned this book to heal, strengthen, equip, and instruct all who have ears to hear what the Spirit of God is speaking today to His people.

Appreciation and love to my exhorters and encouragers while I was writing this book: Lana Garner, Deborah Fairchild, Linda Meyers, Karen Robertson, Sandy Larson, Doris West. Only God knows my appreciation for your prayers, support, and love.

Thank you to Cynthia Lang for your willing heart, your long hours of editing; and for allowing God to pour His wisdom through you into this book.

Contents

Introduction

This book is commissioned by the Holy Spirit to impart, inspire, encourage, and empower His people to advance and fulfill their God-ordained purpose and destiny.

It will help equip and mature people in the prophetic. It will show how the prophetic works to build, edify, encourage, and strengthen the Body of Christ. This is a book for those who have questions regarding the prophetic gifting.

It is meant to help everyone. I hope it will set you free, give insight, and guard you from mistakes in the prophetic. You will learn to recognize the true prophetic voice under the direction of the Holy Spirit. It is a prophetic instruction manual. I will share successes as well as mistakes from 30 years of experience ministering in the prophetic. It will stir up a hunger, desire, and love in the hearts of people to hear God correctly and accurately. My desire is to help purify and clarify the prophetic voice for today. This is meant to be a "prepare ye the way of the Lord"-style book.

The prophet Joel prophesied that in the last days, "*...I will pour out My Spirit upon all flesh; and your sons and your daughters shall prophesy, your old men shall dream dreams, your young men shall see visions: and also upon the servants and upon the handmaids in those days will I pour out My Spirit*" (Joel 2:28-29).

I have included a workbook in the back of the book designed to emphasize the important key aspects of the prophetic. The questions may stimulate further reflection about how you can embrace the prophetic and learn all that God would have you know about this special gifting.

It is extremely imperative to be astute and to discern activities in the supernatural realm. I hope this book will speak to people of all ages whether prophecy is new and fresh to them or they have had many years of experience. There is a need for greater enlightenment and revelation for the prophetic to achieve a higher measure of excellence. We all need to be vigilant to recognize and hear the voice of God.

CHAPTER 1

The Calling

HEAVEN MARKED THIS PLACE

It was a warm summer night in August and a breeze filled the air. Earlier that morning I had been sitting in the middle of my bed with my Bible opened to Psalms.

> *Make a joyful noise unto the Lord, all ye lands. Serve the Lord with gladness: come before His presence with singing. Know ye that the Lord He is God: it is He that hath made us, and not we our selves; we are His people, and the sheep of His pasture. Enter into His gates with thanksgiving, and into His courts with praise: be thankful unto Him, and bless His name. For the Lord is good; His mercy is everlasting; and His truth endureth to all generations* (Psalm 100).

Singing this psalm aloud to the Lord, just as David would have done, had now become part of my prayer life. After my son, Michael; daughter, Theresa; and husband, Fred were off for their daily activities, I would, with great anticipation and expectation, close myself off into my bedroom, which had become my private sanctuary. There I entered into long, sweet unbroken precious hours lost in worship, as I sought the face and voice of my Beloved. Unbeknownst to me, I was being prepared. It was a time of training and listening very closely and intently in order to recognize the voice of the Lord. I was about to practice in public what I was being trained to do in private.

Each Friday night Fred and I joined friends for a time of praise, worship, teaching, and prayer. We met in our church's youth center, an old, small white building that seemed tiny in comparison to the huge church sanctuary and large red brick elementary school. Even though it seemed insignificant and swallowed up by its surroundings, this place had been marked by Heaven for many visitations of His divine presence. Within many of those visitations would be exciting surprises like the one on this August night.

FAST TRACK

As I stepped into the well used and somewhat worn-out room, a feeling of comfort came upon me, just as if I had put on my favorite old slippers. There was a stirring and anticipation. Looking around, I saw smiling faces, old as well as young. The casual surroundings included comfy, overstuffed couches and hard gray metal chairs. We were so grateful to have an old piano and a young man leading us into worship along with his sister on her guitar. Familiar songs such as "Amazing Grace" and "Alleluia" filled the air, as we became one voice full of love and adoration to Jesus our King. We lavished worship on Jesus and declared His authority, singing with all our might, "He is Lord, He is Lord. He has risen from the dead and He is Lord. Every knee shall bow...." Heaven was not only in full agreement, but had initiated this cry from our hearts.

I had only been a part of this group for about eight weeks, yet the surroundings and the service felt familiar and comfortable. In fact, I had accepted Jesus as my personal Lord and Savior just ten weeks prior. I now know Heaven is very familiar with the term "fast track." I was on His fast track and had no idea where I was going or where I would end up. Fred and I sat ready, willing, and open. What to expect...we were not sure. We did know one very important thing— God was more than just in control, He was plotting and preparing the way. We rested in this fact.

The meeting began as usual. One of the leaders taught what he had gleaned from God's Word during the past week so that we all received fresh, hot manna from Heaven. Next, prayer requests were accepted, and the group was eager and willing to agree in prayer with each other. Common threads of love, support, and agreement held this prayer group together. It was known to be a very safe setting where people could feel free to grow in God's Word and in their Christian walk.

> *Behold, how good and how pleasant it is for brethren to dwell together in unity! It is like the precious ointment upon the head that ran down upon the beard, even Aaron's beard: that went down to the skirts of his garments. As the dew of Hermon, and as the dew that descended upon the mountains of Zion: for there the Lord commanded the blessing, even life forevermore* (Psalm 133:1-3).

On this night, that safe setting was about to be tested.

TOTALLY BEWILDERED

As the meeting was coming to an end, we all stood and joined hands in a circle. With one heart and one voice, we were singing the "Our Father" to close the meeting. But wait—there was a surprise. I felt within myself a godly presence of authority—familiar, just like what I had experienced while seeking the heart of God alone in my bedroom. But now, here I stood in front of all these people. I began to repeat the few words that kept coming to my mind. These words became a distraction, and I fought to drown them out. I didn't know why this was happening. At first, I just sang louder and louder, but the words inside my spirit were getting stronger and stronger. They were turning into a burning desire to open my mouth and speak them out. I tightened my lips, because I thought this was not the time nor place for this to be happening. But, just as I decided to say nothing, I heard these same words hang in the air. Yes, I had spoken them! The words were put out there, not to be taken back—gracious words to encourage all whose ears they fell upon. I felt confused and totally bewildered by what had just happened.

The room grew extremely quiet. One could have heard a pin drop; at the same time, I sensed each person straining to hear what had just been spoken. Then I thought, *It's no big deal, just a very nice pretty prayer.* As far as I was concerned, it was a onetime event. I was about to get my cookies and coffee and move back into my comfort zone.

I did not understand that an invasion, a change, had come into my life. Little did I know that what God had planted in me in my secret bedroom sanctuary was now being poured out in public. There was a sense of raw vulnerability, as if someone had taken my very own personal diary and love letters from God and was now reading them in public. Some of the same words—such as "I love you, you are Mine, I've called you by name"—that only I had heard in private, were now being placed in the hearts of others. In my times of communion with Him, He had spoken as through the Song of Solomon: *"Draw me, we will run after Thee: the king hath brought me into His chambers: we will be glad and rejoice in Thee, we will remember Thy love more than wine: the upright love Thee"* (Song of Sol. 1:4). I wasn't quite sure I was willing to share my hidden secrets—God's treasured, deeply intimate words. I wondered whether sharing the words would diminish their sacred value to me. I had secretly guarded His voice, which had built up, encouraged, and taught me. To this point, I had shared my journals of treasured words from Heaven only with my husband, Fred, because with him I felt safe and comfortable. What had just happened in the prayer group left me feeling unsafe and uncomfortable. I was beginning to realize that this was no longer just about me, but about everyone. I saw and felt the response of hurting people's hearts. I knew it was more about them; at the same time, it was still about me.

As I was picking up my much sought after cookie, one of the leaders strolled over to me and excitedly said, "That was one of the most awesome prophecies I have ever heard!"

With an expression of confusion and a strong feeling of bewilderment, I replied, innocently and naively, "What's a prophecy?"

He said, "It is one of the gifts of the Holy Spirit."

I asked, "It's a what?"

Then he opened his Bible and read to me:

But the manifestation of the Spirit is given to each one for the profit of all: for to one is given the word of wisdom through the Spirit, to another the word of knowledge through the same Spirit, to another faith by the same Spirit, to another gifts of healings by the same Spirit, to another the working of miracles, to another prophecy, to another discerning of spirits, to another different kinds of tongues, to another the interpretation of tongues. But one and the same Spirit works all these things, distributing to each one individually as He wills (1 Corinthians 12:7-11 NKJV).

A GREAT START

After reading this to me, he laughed and walked away smiling. So began the great career of God's confused mouthpiece. Like many of God's mouthpieces of the past, I too was off to a "great start." Deep in my heart, I thought this would be a onetime, short, bittersweet experience. Now, after delivering thousands upon thousands of prophecies through the years, I realize that God changes people's plans and puts them into His destiny for them. Prophecy is one of the tools He uses to do this within us.

Had I known in advance what God was going to pour out of me that night, I probably would have stayed hidden at home—safe and happy living my life, just me and my Lord. When He sees a need in one of His children, He places a pull and demand upon His gift within us. The gift is not for building our kingdom or ministry, but *His.* Today, I look back and understand what He spoke to me in regard to ministry: "People are not a vehicle to have a ministry, but ministry is a vehicle to help people, to love and serve them." "*The manifestation of the Spirit is given to each one for the profit of all...*" (1 Cor. 12:7 NKJV).

Heavenly Father,

I ask You to draw me into Your very presence, to seek Your face and to hear Your voice. Please help me to put aside all unnecessary distractions and demands. I want a heart like that of King David, who followed hard after You. Take my whole heart, mind, and will. I surrender my entire self…I long to have a secret place in You.

Father, in the powerful name of Jesus, my Lord and Savior, and by the Holy Spirit, I believe and meditate on Psalm 91:1 NKJV: "_____ [your name] who dwells in the secret place of the Most High shall abide under the shadow of the Almighty."

In the precious name of Jesus, Amen.

MEDITATION

Ask the Father in Jesus' name: "Lord, I come before You and ask You to make known to me the gift(s) deposited in me according to First Corinthians 1:7-11."

MEDITATION SCRIPTURE

But the manifestation of the Spirit is given to each one for the profit of all: for to one is given the word of wisdom through the Spirit, to another the word of knowledge through the same Spirit, to another faith by the same Spirit, to another gifts of healings by the same Spirit, to another the working of miracles, to another prophecy, to another discerning of spirits, to another different kinds of tongues, to another the interpretation of tongues. But one and the same Spirit works all these things, distributing to each one individually as He wills (1 Corinthians 12:7-11).

Devotional

Key Scriptures: Psalm 100; Psalm 133; Joel 2:28-29; 1 Corinthians 12:7-11; Song of Solomon 1:4.

Key Point: It was a time of training and listening very closely and intently in order to recognize the voice of the Lord. I was about to practice in public what I was being trained to do in private.

HEAVEN MARKED THIS PLACE

1. What should you do to clearly hear the voice of the Lord?

   a. Worship
   b. Desire unbroken, intimate fellowship
   c. Seek God's face
   d. Retreat to a private sanctuary
   e. Listen
   f. All of the above

FAST TRACK

2. What requirements should you look for in a group to help you develop your calling?

TOTALLY BEWILDERED

3. "I felt within myself a godly presence of _____."

4. "At first, I just sang louder and louder, but the words inside my spirit were getting _____ and _____."

A GREAT START

5. What can God use to change people's plans to put them into His destiny for them?

_____

_____

6. "People are not a vehicle to have ministry, but ministry is a vehicle to help people." True or False?

CHAPTER 2

Prophets of Old

SIGNIFICANCE OF A NAME

Many of the prophets of old didn't understand or even want to be called. Jeremiah was called at a young age. *"Then the word of the Lord came to me, saying: 'Before I formed you in the womb I knew you; before you were born I sanctified you; I ordained you a prophet to the nations'"*(Jer. 1:4-5 NKJV). Jeremiah's name means "exalted of God" and yet he was called the "weeping prophet." Ezekiel, Jeremiah's younger contemporary, was in his mid-twenties, training to become a priest, and looking forward to serving in the temple as had his father before him. Exile in the plains of Babylonia, far from Jerusalem, meant the end of all his hopes. But again, God reached down and called him into service as a prophet. *"And He said to me, 'Son of man, stand on your feet, and I will speak to you.' Then the Spirit entered me when He spoke to me, and set me on my feet; and I heard Him who spoke to me"* (Ezek. 2:1-2 NKJV).

True to his name, *Ezekiel* means "the strength of God." Many today are like Joel, who is "the unknown one." We only know Joel's father's name, Pethuel. (See Joel 1:1.) Joel's name literally means "Jehovah is God." It is interesting that in the Book of Joel, the unknown prophet, God promises, *"And it shall come to pass afterward that I will pour out My Spirit on all flesh; your sons and your daughters shall prophesy, your old men shall dream dreams, your young men shall see visions. And also on My menservants and on My maidservants I will pour out My Spirit in those days"* (Joel 2:28-29 NKJV).

Apparently, the meaning of names is extremely significant to God. Jesus turned water into wine. He likewise turned *Simon*, which meant "stone or pebble" into *Peter*, a "massive rock." This was a prophetic name that was yet to be fulfilled in Peter's lifetime.

When God calls someone, it is very evident He calls that person at a certain time, a certain place, to give a certain message to a certain group of people. Not all mouthpieces of God prophesied the outpouring of God's Spirit. There was a common theme of calling people back to God in order to repent, receive His love, and grow in relationship with Him. Some, like Isaiah whose name means "salvation of Jehovah," answered the call.

> *I saw also the Lord sitting upon a throne, high and lifted up, and His train filled the temple. Above it stood the seraphims: each one had six wings; with twain, he covered his face, and with twain he covered his feet, and with twain he did fly. And one cried unto another, and said, Holy, holy, holy is the Lord of Hosts: the whole earth is full of His glory. And the posts of the door moved at the voice of him that cried, and the house was filled with smoke. Then said I, woe is me! for I am undone; because I am a man of unclean lips, and I dwell in the midst of a people of unclean lips: for mine eyes have seen the King, the Lord of Hosts....Also I heard the voice of the Lord, saying, Whom shall I send, and who will go for Us? Then said I, Here am I; send me"* (Isaiah 6:1-5,8).

The Bible repeatedly shows God's prophets calling rebellious people to repentance and restoration, because of His love and faithfulness—not because of their loyalty. The Word says, "Or do you despise the riches of His goodness, forbearance, and longsuffering, not knowing that the goodness of God leads you to repentance?" (Rom. 2:4 NKJV)

THE RUNAWAY PROPHET

Then there was Jonah, who, upon receiving the call of God to preach to the people of Nineveh, ran away from the Lord. *"But Jonah arose to flee to Tarshish from the presence of the Lord. He went down to Joppa, and found a ship going to Tarshish; so he paid the fare [trying to buy his way out of his call], and went down into it, to go with them to Tarshish from the presence of the Lord"* (Jon. 1:3 NKJV).

In fairness to Jonah, he had not seen a glorious vision of the Lord like Isaiah had seen. But Isaiah recognized that God was sending him to disobedient people. Jonah also knew that God was sending him to cruel people who loved their rebellion. Perhaps he looked forward to seeing these people wiped off the face of the earth—while conveniently disregarding his own rebellion.

In His mercy, God gave both the citizens of Nineveh and Jonah a second chance. Jonah's second chance to answer his call came after he was locked up in the smelly, dark, scary belly of a whale. Did Jonah discover the Mediterranean diet? Only God knows! Jonah started out on his own mission, which was to go in the opposite direction from where God had called him to go. In spite of Jonah's willfulness, Heaven triumphed in the end. This story could have had a very different and disastrous ending—not only for Jonah, but also for those he was sent to deliver.

SEND ME, LORD

In looking at these prophets, we find that how they answered their calls and lived them out differed in many ways. Today, God is still seeking after those who are from different stations in life and talents. He longs for those who will respond like Isaiah, with a willing and obedient, "Send me, Lord." Just as God did yesterday, He is still looking at the motives of those he calls. God is looking for those with a heart like Amos, whose name means "burden bearer." Even though he was a layman and a shepherd, Amos's heart was so close to God that 40 times in his prophecies he states, "This is what the Lord says." Today, perhaps even more than in the days of Amos, God's mouthpieces should be able to say, with authority, purity, and truth, "This is what the Lord says."

We must be willing to accept the responsibility that His name carries, in order for the recipient to receive the right message. Just as a mail carrier must deliver a letter with accuracy and efficiency, the prophetic voice must be precise and timely in order to be fully delivered in the most excellent manner. It's a far greater responsibility for a prophetic vessel to deliver God's messages to His people, than for a mail carrier to deliver a person-to-person message.

Next we will look at some of the things that can either help or hinder us in clearly hearing the voice of the Lord.

Heavenly Father,

I thank You that Your Word says, "Before I formed you in the womb, I knew you." I ask You to clearly make known to me the plans and purposes You have designed for my life. Father, please never let me flee from Your will, but instead embrace it. I know You are the great God of second chances. If I have strayed from Your path, please bring me back. I ask You now to place me in Your highest will and to put Your grace in my heart, enabling me to be sent by You and not by man or myself. Prepare me to become a mouthpiece. Please fill my mouth with Your words.

In Jesus' wonderful name, Amen.

MEDITATION SCRIPTURE

Let the words of my mouth and the meditation of my heart be acceptable in Your sight, O Lord, my strength and my Redeemer (Psalm 19:14 NKJV).

Devotional

Key Scriptures: Jeremiah 1:4-5; Ezekiel 2:1-2; Joel 1:1; Joel 2:28-29; Romans 2:4; Isaiah 6:1-5,8; Jonah 1:3.

Key Point: Today, perhaps even more than in the days of Amos, God's mouthpieces should be able to say, with authority, purity, and truth, "This is what the Lord says."

SIGNIFICANCE OF A NAME

1. Who is the "unknown prophet"?

   _____

2. "When God calls someone, it is very evident He calls him or her at a _____, a _____, to give a _____, to a _____."

3. What are the common themes of God's messages?

   a. Repentance
   b. Receiving God's love
   c. Growing in relationship with God
   d. Moving out of rebellion
   e. All of the above

THE RUNAWAY PROPHET

4. When answering his call, Jonah saw a glorious vision like Isaiah did. True or False?

SEND ME, LORD

5. "God's mouthpieces should be able to say, with authority, purity and truth, '_____'."

CHAPTER 3

Who's Speaking Now?

TEST THE FRUIT

It is very important to test and taste the fruit of prophecy, which can deposit either life or death. You test a prophecy by looking at the fruit that is born from the words. Even when God sees people in rebellion that leads them to death, He still desires to produce and author words of life to them. Jesus said:

> *You will know them by their fruits. Do men gather grapes from thornbushes or figs from thistles? Even so, every good tree bears good fruit, but a bad tree bears bad fruit. A good tree cannot bear bad fruit, nor can a bad tree bear good fruit. Every tree that does not bear good fruit is cut down and thrown into the fire. Therefore by their fruits you will know them* (Matthew 7:16-20 NKJV).

He did not say, "You will know them by their *gifts*."

Jesus warns us of false prophets. It is exciting to know He is telling us how to recognize the true prophetic. The counterfeit can only be forged from the original. God originated the gift of prophecy; it came from His holiness and purity. The true prophetic carries the highest and most valuable cost, so we must treasure it. It should edify, encourage, and strengthen. It should only be brought by the Holy Spirit, who is the Spirit of truth. After a true word of prophecy, an observer should be able to see life imparted into a situation. It should produce hope where there was no hope; direction where there was confusion; bring peace where there was turbulence; and healing where there was brokenness or sickness.

HEART MOTIVES

Today, many people who claim to be hearing the voice of the Lord give words that seem to have come from the same heart that was in Jonah. Those who speak for Him should exhibit the same kind of love that the apostle John spoke of and lived by: "*Beloved, do not believe every spirit, but test the spirits, whether they are of God; because many false prophets have gone out into the world*" (1 John 4:1 NKJV).

From days of old until now, false voices have always existed with the ones God has raised up to carry His voice to a hurting world. God is concerned with the heart motives of the people He calls. He desires His voice to be declared from hearts full of love for His creation. Just as Jesus spoke and walked in truth—but always with compassion—so should those who carry the prophetic voice. "*And though I have the gift of prophecy, and understand all mysteries and all knowledge, and though I have all faith, so that I could remove mountains, but have not love, I am nothing*" (1Cor. 13:2 NKJV).

A SURE WORD

We are cautioned and encouraged to grow in the gifts God has placed in us to release the Kingdom of God on earth. The apostle Paul encouraged Timothy, "*Do not neglect the gift that is in you, which was given to you by prophecy with the laying on of the hands of the eldership*" (1 Tim. 4:14 NKJV). Timothy was encouraged to grow into hearing a sure word of prophecy. As people who are longing to hear the voice of the Lord and declare it, we should make sure we are able to say, "Thus saith the Lord" after we have spoken a word in His name. As it is stated, "*And so we have the prophetic word confirmed, which you do well to heed as a light that shines in a dark place, until the day dawns and the morning star rises in your hearts*" (2 Pet. 1:19 NKJV).

It is very important that our hearts remain pure, so that the words we utter into others' lives will have the stamp of the Holy Spirit upon them. A true prophetic word must not have our will stamped on it. The truth of the matter is, our will is irrelevant and of no importance compared to God's will in relation to people. *"For prophecy never came by the will of man, but holy men of God spoke as they were moved by the Holy Spirit"* (2 Pet. 1:21 NKJV). We have a choice—to be motivated and moved by the Holy Spirit, or to draw out of our own flesh words that are not from the heart of God. We must guard against our own soulish motives, words that stem from pride, when we speak to fill our egos like the false prophets did. The Old Testament shows how these prophets told kings exactly what they wanted to hear, to garner favor for their own personal gain.

TEST THE SPIRITS

First Kings tells of a king of Israel who was thinking of going into battle. Having received a promise of military support from Judah's king, Jehoshaphat, the king of Israel then consulted his prophets.

> *Then the king of Israel gathered the prophets together, about four hundred men, and said to them, "Shall I go against Ramoth Gilead to fight, or shall I refrain?" So they said, "Go up, for the Lord will deliver it into the hand of the king."....And all the prophets prophesied so, saying, "Go up to Ramoth Gilead and prosper, for the Lord will deliver it into the king's hand"* (1 Kings 22:6,12 NKJV).

The king of Israel had a problem. Instead of testing the spirit behind the words, he simply listened to these prophets who tickled his ears with promises of victory and power. The visiting King Jehoshaphat, however, asked the king of Israel, *"Please inquire for the word of the Lord today"* (1 Kings 22:5 NKJV). Clearly Jehoshaphat recognized that the 400 prophets were not true prophets of God, but were prophets of the land. Such individuals are usually ambitious for land, power, or position for themselves. Prophets of the Lord prophesy His word and stand against other voices of strange prophets. The king of Israel reluctantly said, *"There is still one man, Micaiah the son of Imlah, by whom we may inquire of the Lord; but I hate him, because he does not prophesy good concerning me, but evil"* (1 Kings 22:8 NKJV).

Prophesying truth does not guarantee that the prophet will be loved and accepted at all times. In fact, sometimes speaking forth God's direction and plan will collide head on with man's schemes and plans. As a result, hate and unjust anger may be directed toward the prophet in spite of the fact that he carries the voice of the Lord. In this age, prophetic people have a choice—stand solid in the word of the Lord, or run for the cave and hide.

DO NOT DESPISE PROPHECY

First Thessalonians 5:20 says, *"Do not despise prophecies"* (NKJV). First Samuel 15 tells how King Saul despised true prophecy and because of this, he threw open the doors to bring in false prophets. They were able to give him multiple false visions and false prophecies. He opened the door for a lying spirit to enter in, set up, and bring forth destruction. *"For rebellion is as the sin of witchcraft, and stubbornness is as iniquity and idolatry. Because thou hast rejected the word of the Lord* [prophecy], *He has also rejected thee from being king"* (1 Sam. 15:23). Disregarding prophecy, whether on a national or individual scale, can lead to grave and deadly circumstances. *"And the Lord said to me, 'The prophets prophesy lies in My name. I have not sent them, commanded them, nor spoken to them; they prophesy to you a false vision, divination, a worthless thing, and the deceit of their heart'"* (Jer. 14:14 NKJV). It seems to be God in His goodness, mercy, and love honors the free will of an individual as well as the choice of a nation. The safeguard against the activity of a lying spirit is to stay in submission to the voice and the will of God. God's will is heard through His written Word, the inner witness, or through the voice of His prophets.

We must recognize who is sending whom, and we must discern if there is any deceit in our own hearts as well as theirs. We go back to what I said earlier; we must be able to know and perceive if it is the Lord speaking or that of man. There are some who prophesy in their own name, from their own hearts, and for their own personal gain—at the expense of the personal pain of others. Others are sent and called by the Lord to prophesy and establish His words for His people on the earth.

DECLARE HIS HEART

Some words will tickle your ears; some words will cause you to grow in vanity. We are warned: *"Do not listen to the words of the prophets who prophesy to you. They make you worthless; they speak a vision of their own heart, not from the mouth of the Lord"* (Jer. 23:16 NKJV). As stated earlier, it is absolutely crucial to recognize which mouthpieces belong to the Lord and which ones are counterfeit. It goes back to whose orders they are operating under—Heaven's or some other spirit's? God clearly states in His Word that His prophets are called and set apart to know His will. The reason they can declare His words is because they have their ears to His heart. They are listening intently to recognize His voice and to speak only what they have heard. *" 'Behold, I am against those who prophesy false dreams,' says the Lord, 'and tell them, and cause My people to err by their lies and by their recklessness. Yet I did not send them or command them; therefore they shall not profit this people at all,' says the Lord"* (Jer. 23:32 NKJV). We should all guard our hearts from vanity and rebellion. We need to have within us the ability to recognize and discern the words of the Spirit of God. We must know beyond a shadow of a doubt whose spirit is behind the words. Learn to recognize and discern the effect of word of prophecy and what has been deposited in the lives and situations of those who received it. Has it brought forth division or unity? Has it caused pain, grief, and sorrow—or has it established joy, freedom, and hope? Our God is truly a God who loves His people. We must all guard against prophesying out of our own hearts, which may be deceitful and can hurt the very people that God has called us to love. True prophecy always declares God's heart.

31

Heavenly Father,

I ask You to help me test the gift of prophecy in my life. If I am holding on to any prophetic word that has not been given to me by the Holy Spirit, please break the power of that word. Jesus, You are my Beloved. Please help me to grow in faith "agreement" with every prophetic word You have spoken over me. Please fill me with Your love for myself and others. Let all pride and hidden agendas I may have in my heart die now. Grant me the ability to discern the words of Your Holy Spirit from this day forward. Grow me up in the ways of Your Kingdom, for I know I belong to You.

In Jesus' name, Amen.

MEDITATION SCRIPTURE

There is no fear in love, but perfect love casts out fear, because fear involves torment. But he who fears has not been made perfect in love. We love Him because He first loved us (1 John 4:18-19 NKJV).

Devotional

Key Scriptures: Matthew 7:16-20; 1 John 4:1; 1 Corinthians 13:2; 1 Timothy 4:14; 2 Peter 1:19, 21; 1 Kings 22:5-12; 1 Thessalonians 5:20; 1 Samuel 15:23; Jeremiah 14:14; Jeremiah 23:16; Jeremiah 23:32.

Key Point: We need to have within us the ability to recognize and discern the words of the Spirit of God. We must know beyond a shadow of a doubt, whose spirit is behind the words.

TEST THE FRUIT

1. "It is very important to test and taste the fruit of prophecy, which can deposit either _____ or _____."

2. The true prophetic should deposit which three results?

   _____

   _____

   _____

3. Who originated prophecy?
   a. God
   b. Man
   c. Woman
   d. Abraham

HEART MOTIVES

4. "Beloved, do not believe every _____ , but test the _____ whether they are of God because many false _____ have gone out into the world" (1 John 4:1 NKJV).

A SURE WORD

5. Which method was used to impart a gift to Timothy?
   a. Laying on of hands
   b. By prophecy
   c. Baptizing with water
   d. Fasting and prayer
   e. a and b

6. "We must guard against our own _____ _____."

TEST THE SPIRITS

7. There was another king of Judah, Jehoshaphat, who inquired from the king of Israel, David. True or False?

8. What are the differences between the prophets of the land and the prophets of the Lord?

_____

_____

_____

DO NOT DESPISE PROPHECY

9. King Saul despised true prophecy and because of this, he threw open the doors to bring in victory in battle/ false prophets/, prosperity/ indigestion. (Circle one.)

10. "The safeguard against the activity of a lying spirit is to
    _____ to the _____ and the
    _____."

DECLARE HIS HEART

11. We are warned: "Do not listen to the words of the prophets who
    prophesy to you. They make you _____; they speak a
    _____ of their own _____, not from _____"
    (Jer. 23:16 NKJV).

CHAPTER 4

In the Hot Seat

A Test in Disguise

Years ago while attending a Christian Spirit-filled retreat for thousands of leaders in New Mexico, we experienced many wonderful moments as God's Spirit moved and manifested His tangible presence.

One night, I was so looking forward to being placed in the "hot seat" in one of the workshops, which means having people pray over you the words of the Lord. Now I was new to the things of the Spirit; it was my first year of walking closely with the Spirit. He was developing the gift of discerning of spirits, and His lessons were about to become a test in disguise.

We were assigned to a group of unknown people to pray over us. I soon found myself in a circle staring at the "hot seat," a lone chair placed in the center of the circle that dared me to occupy it. The chair alone was very intimidating and threatening, because of the strangers standing around the perimeter staring at me. The whole scenario was both inviting and challenging, as the unknown many times is. I felt like the chair had a secret, as if it were aware of the trauma we were about to encounter.

The man and woman who led this small group beckoned each one of us to come sit in the "hot seat," so they could pray over us what they felt God was telling them to pray. I began to squirm uneasily as I heard what they prayed over the first person and watched her painful, tearful response. In order to settle into my own chair, I kept telling myself, *Do not judge.* For the Word says, *"Judge not, and ye shall not be judged; condemn not, and ye shall not be condemned: forgive and ye shall be forgiven"* (Luke 6:37). Yet the more I silently repeated these words, the more anxiety flooded my heart. I found myself in the middle of a battle that I had not expected at a prayer meeting. I sat by silently as the leaders prayed over their first "casualty." I remember it as if it were yesterday. She was a young woman of approximately 30 years old with dull, sandy brown hair and very sad, blank eyes. Her small shoulders were slightly bent over, as though she carried the weight of a terrible burden. She began to tell the sad story of having adopted a baby two years prior—and now finding herself unable to love this child. The tears rolled off her cheeks and fell on the white handkerchief she held tightly wrapped around her fingers.

I fought back tears, wishing I could hold her in my arms and bring reassurance and hope to her. However, I was not the leader, so I stayed in submission, just plain fidgeting. I reluctantly listened as they continued to pray. One said, "The reason she is not able to love the child is that the birth mother still holds the child with soul ties. If the natural mother won't let go, she will never be free to love the child." At this, the young woman's sobs grew even stronger and her body began to tremble as if she were in great agony. She seemed to be wrapped in a blanket of hopelessness. *"Hope deferred maketh the heart sick"* (Prov. 13:12a). I could hardly contain myself, for my silence felt that it was lending agreement to a lie, yet I remained still.

GET UP AND PRAY

The Holy Spirit, who was also listening to the judgmental prayers, challenged me, "That is not true! I want you to stand up, pray truth, and speak a word that will set her free."

I countered, "I'm not in charge."

He firmly replied, "I AM."

I was beginning to feel like Moses arguing with God at the burning bush! *"Moses said unto God, 'Who am I, that I should go unto Pharaoh, and that I should bring forth the children of Israel out of Egypt?'...And*

God said unto Moses, 'I AM THAT I AM': and He said, 'Thus shalt thou say unto the children of Israel, I AM hath sent me unto you'" (Exod. 3:11,14). I felt intimidated, just like Moses. Still I sat silently listening.

At this point the other leader, a thin balding man who seemed very sincere, said, "We must take authority, and bind this spirit that is causing you to be so angry and hurt that you are unable to give love to this child." The young lady's body, wracked with sobs, just folded over helplessly as layer upon layer of hopelessness, judgment, and condemnation were piled on her. The leaders smiled one to another, probably thinking they had heard God. When they had finished praying for this young woman, the heaviness on her actually seemed to have doubled in proportion. She politely thanked them and with a devastated look slowly returned to her seat, slumping down in her chair. Once again I heard the Holy Spirit say, "I want you to pray over these people." Yet I remained still. After all, I rationalized, I was merely an attendee learning to recognize the voice of God.

PLAYING IT SAFE

Victim number two was a young cleric about 35 years old. Although he was handsome and rugged looking, discouragement was written all over his face. He dropped heavily into the "hot seat." Heartbroken for what I had just witnessed with the young woman, I was extremely agitated by what I suspected might happen again.

No sooner had he hit the chair when he too crumbled and burst into uncontrollable tears. I felt that I was being forced to watch an emotional beating, helpless to intervene. Finally, with every ounce of courage and respect within me, I asked permission to pray quickly over him. I nervously awaited the leaders' response. They glared at me with astonishment and intense judgment, yet reluctantly agreed to let me pray. I had two choices—either resist the strong, relentless conviction of the Holy Spirit, or stand up and face the intimidating glares of the leaders. This Scripture flashed through my mind: *"And when they bring you unto the synagogues, and unto magistrates, and powers, take ye no thought how or what thing ye shall answer, or what ye shall say: for the Holy Ghost shall teach you in the same hour what ye ought to say"* (Luke 12:11-12).

Quietly and gently, as the Holy Spirit flowed through me, I began to pray. Using extreme caution, He showed me how vulnerable and deeply heartbroken this young man was. With His authority and assurance I said, "God Himself is calling you to the mountains to come and seek His face. When you do this, He is going to renew you, refresh you, and refill you. As you respond to God's call, He will give you the ability and strategy to love and heal people." The words seemed innocent enough to me.

His crying became more intense. Now his tears became tears of joy! He meekly looked up and asked, "May I share with you?"

The leaders were slow in responding and most anxious to see how my test would come out. I merely nodded my agreement...after all, I wasn't in charge. The man in the hot seat told us he was a priest who had come down from Canada and was thinking of leaving the priesthood. He could no longer love and care for his congregation or be under the burden of serving God.

He continued, "I came here to give God a last chance to speak to me. Tomorrow, I am going to the mountains. I have my hiking boots, for I had planned to go away to hear the voice of God." With this, he cried with joy and relief. Beyond a shadow of a doubt, he knew that God had a divine appointment waiting for him. His radiant face registered the peace that flooded his entire being. He now knew he could respond to the love of God.

I smiled inside, knowing that this was at least one time I had been obedient to the Spirit of the Lord. So I began to humble myself even more, or so I thought.

THE PAYBACK

Reluctantly, I asked the leaders to pray for me so I could be used more by God. I took my place in the tormenting "hot seat." Things did not go well for me.

The lady prayed, "Lord, crush her and destroy her until there is nothing left."

And the man said, "Amen."

I guess it was payback time. Apparently they didn't like me because, under the anointing of the Holy Ghost, I had undone what they had prayed over poor, hurting innocent people. Listening to their prayers, I cried out in my spirit, begging God not to answer their request. I politely thanked them, leaped off the "hot seat," and found my place back in the circle. At this point, I still felt very intimidated by them. I had watched and heard what they had spoken and done to the others. I felt blessed to get away with my spirit, soul, and body still intact.

At the time I did not realize that God was breaking the fear of man off me. Particularly for those who operate in the prophetic, this issue can be a major stumbling block and extremely crippling. "*The fear of man bringeth a snare: but whoso putteth his trust in the Lord shall be safe*" (Prov. 29:25).

A SECOND CHANCE

My heart was still heavy for the young mother, who had been vulnerable and poured out her heart of pain only to receive condemnation and judgment. So I began to pray, "Lord, please forgive me for not being brave and obedient; please allow me to make up for my disobedience." In my heart, I desperately wanted God to give me a second chance, just as He had done for Jonah.

Later that night, after the meeting ended, it was still quite warm outside. I could hardly find my way along the path because of the darkness. Suddenly, I tripped over something—or rather, *someone!* This very same young mother from the prayer circle sat on the curb, with her husband's arms wrapped around her in his attempt to console her. Among the thousands of people at this conference, I had stumbled upon this young woman. I knew God had mercifully answered my prayer and had given me a second chance to pray for her. Gently I explained that earlier the Lord had shown me what she needed and how to pray. Would she mind if I prayed with her now? With eyes still filled with pain and anguish, she consented. The essence of my prayer and words was that God knew she was unable at this point to love her child. Instead of judging her, He had come this night to fill her with His own love for the child. Because He trusted her to intercede, He had handpicked her to become the mother to love, pray, and cherish this child. There was a high calling on this young one. The Lord wanted to reassure her that she would be able not only to raise the child in His ways, but to love him with God's love, beyond her own ability.

Immediately, the tears of sorrow and pain turned into tears of joy. "*In His favor is life: weeping may endure for a night, but joy cometh in the morning*" (Ps. 30:5b). The Lord Himself truly does heal the broken-hearted and set the captives free.

> *The Spirit of the Lord is upon Me, because He hath anointed Me to preach the gospel to the poor; He hath sent Me to heal the broken-hearted, to preach deliverance to the captives, and recovering of sight to the blind, to set at liberty them that are bruised, to preach the acceptable year of the Lord* (Luke 4:18-19).

God in His knowledge and wisdom had trusted the young mother with this child's destiny, so he could fulfill his purpose in God. Our God truly is a good God, a fact that He was about to prove to me within the next 24 hours.

Heavenly Father,

> *Please take from me the need and desire to please all people at all times. Break off the fear of man that can lead me into disobeying You. I truly want to be free from all "man pleasing" and be in total obedience to You now and always. Help me not to look or listen to the left or to the right by seeking man's approval. Father, help me to be like Jesus, who only did what You showed Him to do. Please pull me out of any snare of man I am in or have been in. Make me bold to follow You...love You...and love Your precious people.*

> *In Jesus' name I pray, Amen.*

MEDITATION SCRIPTURE

The fear of man bringeth a snare: but whoso putteth his trust in the Lord shall be safe (Proverbs 29:25).

Devotional

Key Scriptures: Luke 6:37; Proverbs 13:12; Exodus 3:11,14; Luke 12:11-12; Proverbs 29:25; Psalm 30:5; Luke 4:18-19.

Key Point: God was developing the gift of discerning of spirits, and His lessons were about to become a test in disguise.

A TEST IN DISGUISE

1. "In order to settle into my own chair, I kept telling myself, You must judge." True or False?

2. "However, I was not the leader, so I stayed in submission/agreement/rebellion, just plain fidgeting." (Circle one.)

GET UP AND PRAY

3. The Holy Spirit, who was also listening to the judgmental prayers, challenged Eileen:

   a. "You have no authority here, so be still."
   b. "Stay in submission and sit down."
   c. "I want you to stand up, pray truth,
      and speak a word that will set her free."
   d. "Now is not the time to release her."
   e. None of the above.

PLAYING IT SAFE

4. Have you ever found yourself in a similar situation; choosing between obeying God and pleasing people? If so, how did you respond?

_____

_____

_____

CHAPTER 5

The Counterfeit Versus the Genuine

An Encounter of the Strange Kind

The very next morning, I was feeling content and happy inside. I knew that my Redeemer lives, for He had proven this the night before. So with a carefree heart and a bounce in my step, I entered a classroom. A great teacher from the 1970s, Dr. Morton Kelsey, was going to explain the gifts of visions and dreams. I was excited to hear how God was going to train and develop me in these greater gifts of revelation. As I surveyed the classroom looking for an empty chair, I saw the lady leader who had prayed over me in the "hot seat" the night before. With well-founded apprehension, I approached her hesitantly. I had an instant flashback to her destructive prayer for me. Not only had she prayed that God would crush me, but she had also shared a vision that scared me.

She had said, "I saw you in a vision. You were a little girl, carefree and happy. You were swinging on a swing, and God was pushing your swing. He was pushing you higher and higher and higher, until you fell off." Her warped interpretation of this so-called vision, crushing and destroying me in order to teach me humility, struck great fear in my heart. *"For God hath not given us the spirit of fear; but of power, and of love, and of a sound mind"* (2 Tim. 1:7).

Now, I knew I hadn't quickly obeyed God in the matter of praying for the young mother, but I really didn't believe He would push me off a swing high in the air and leave me lying injured and helpless on the ground. I had absolutely no desire to speak to this woman or to receive any more "ministry" from her. I just wanted to stay healed and happy.

God had another plan. As I tried to slip by her, I felt a tug on my arm. She smiled brightly with satisfaction, and said pointedly, "I must tell you. In fact, I have to tell you. When I first saw you, I saw your aura. It was a bright green, and your energy field was full of great energy representing healing."

I weakly smiled, reluctantly thanked her, and quickly escaped. Having no idea what she was talking about, I wanted to run away as fast as I could. The night before, I had mentally put her in a box on which I wrote, "Weird and strange—do not open again."

Paul also encountered the "weird and strange" through the operation of counterfeit gifts.

> *Then certain of the vagabond Jews, exorcists, took upon them to call over them which had evil spirits the name of the Lord Jesus, saying, We adjure you by Jesus whom Paul preacheth. And there were seven sons of one Sceva, a Jew, and chief of the priests, which did so. And the evil spirit answered and said, Jesus I know, and Paul I know; but who are ye? And the man in whom the evil spirit was leaped on them, and overcame them, and prevailed against them, so that they fled out of that house naked and wounded* (Acts 19:13-16).

However, Paul clearly operated in the genuine gifts, because God brought special signs, wonders and miracles through him. *"And God wrought special miracles by the hands of Paul: so that from his body were brought unto the sick handkerchiefs or aprons, and the diseases departed from them, and the evil spirits went out of them"* (Acts 19:11-12).

Praise the Lord for His wonderful works through His faithful, true servants!

Two Different Kingdoms

Later that afternoon in prayer, God showed me why I wanted to run from the woman. By the Holy Spirit, I realized that I had stood against a New Age spirit. She was not filled with God's Holy Spirit. We served two different kingdoms. This was a great lesson that taught me discerning of spirits is absolutely essential when you operate in gifts of prophecy or any of the other revelatory gifts. Where the Spirit of the Lord is, there truly is freedom. *"For the kingdom of God is not eating and drinking, but righteousness and peace and joy in the Holy Spirit"* (Rom. 14:17 NKJV).

Jesus warned us of false prophets who would come in sheep's clothing. He told us to be alert and stay vigilant in order to recognize the spirit that is behind the words, visions, or the power that is being manifested. The trouble with being deceived is that the person who is in deception does not know it. What appears good and genuine, in reality is evil at the core. According to *Webster's Dictionary*, the word *deceive* means "to cause to believe an untruth or to use or practice deceit, beguile, betray, delude, or mislead." This is the assignment of the demonic. The Word of God states that satan will come as an angel of light. Satan is a deceiver, robber and distracter. He lures with a false appearance and then deceives with either an all-out lie or a partial truth. *"Ye are of your father the devil, and the lusts of your father ye will do. He was a murderer from the beginning, and abode not in the truth, because there is no truth in him. When he speaketh a lie, he speaketh of his own: for he is a liar, and the father of it"* (John 8:44).

Many of us, being open and desiring to hear the voice of the Lord, live in a state of vulnerability. Living in a state of vulnerability is not a bad thing. In fact, it's a requirement to be open in order to receive from God. We need the wisdom and the Spirit of truth to lead, direct, guide, and to protect and keep us in the truth. Some psychics or prophets operate with a deceitful supernatural power, while claiming to be instruments in the hand of a loving God. If they were to meet the Lord face to face today, they would hear Him say, *"I never knew you: depart from Me, ye that work iniquity"* (Matt. 7:23). Sadly, they do not know Him as their Lord and Savior at all. They've never heard His voice.

BE ON GUARD

The Word says false prophets *shall* arise; not that they *might* arise. This is a definitive statement where God is warning His people. There is no *maybe* about it. Their outer appearance may not necessarily offend you—they may come in acceptable apparel and appealing mannerisms. This is why the Lord warns us to look inwardly at people's hearts; being sure to test the motives and ambitions that lie within them. The Word says, "*Beware* [picture a red light] *of false prophets, which come to you in sheep's clothing, but inwardly they are ravening wolves*" (Matt. 7:15). *Beware* means "to be on one's guard and to be wary of." A red light signals we are to stop, look, and listen.

In other words, we are to test the spirits. We are not merely to blindly accept words, not even what seems innocent and fun in appearance. The bottom line is these people are operating through a spirit to bewitch, just as they tried with the Galatians. "*O foolish Galatians, who hath bewitched you, that ye should not obey the truth, before whose eyes Jesus Christ hath been evidently set forth, crucified among you?*" (Gal. 3:1)

Most of the time, these events do not happen in a dark, scary hole. Instead, they happen openly on a bright sunny day in any public or private situation full of fun and entertainment. It can happen with family, friends, or strangers, because satan comes through any open door where he can gain a foothold. He wants control over you and those you love. He comes into situations that may appear innocent and lighthearted, but he has the same goal: to bring deception and to captivate your life, will, future, and destiny. The definition of *bewitch* is "to affect by witchcraft, charm, fascinate, enchant, attract and captivate." The goal of satan and his cohorts is to trap you into bewitchment.

"*For there shall arise false Christs, and false prophets, and shall show great signs and wonders; insomuch that, if it were possible, they shall deceive the very elect*" (Matt. 24:24). What this means is that false prophets, by their false power, will do amazing things in order to entice, stir up our curiosity, and pull us into their persuasion of deception. In this Scripture, there is one tiny word that stands out above other words—*if.*

Our part is to be on guard and on the look out so that the "ifs" will be warning signals, and we will not be deceived.

How Quickly We Forget

"*And when they say to you, 'Seek those who are mediums and wizards, who whisper and mutter,' should not a people seek their God? Should they seek the dead on behalf of the living?*" (Isa. 8:19 NKJV). This practice is called *necromancy* or speaking to the dead—which is another way of saying, speaking to spirits that are familiar with departed loved ones. Here are the counterfeit and deceptive tactics of the demonic opposing the Holy Spirit and His gifts. The Spirit of God sets us free and points us in the direction of the Lord Jesus Christ.

When the Israelites wanted a visible leader—someone to place their faith in, just as the heathens did, God gave them Saul. By this choice, they not only displeased Samuel (see 1 Sam. 8:6), but they also pushed aside the intimacy of having the Lord God in Heaven rule over them as their King. They turned aside from Heaven's control and chose instead to come under the lordship of man. How quickly the people had forgotten it was the arm of the Lord that brought them out of slavery from the land of the Egyptians. They had become a rebellious people.

> *And the Lord said to Samuel, "Heed the voice of the people in all that they say to you; for they have not rejected you, but they have rejected Me, that I should not reign over them. According to all the works which they have done since the day that I brought them up out of Egypt, even to this day—with which they have forsaken Me and served other gods—so they are doing to you also. Now therefore, heed their voice. However, you shall solemnly forewarn them, and show them the behavior of the king who will reign over them"* (1 Samuel 8:7-9 NKJV).

This was an extremely tragic and sad day for the Lord, Samuel, and Israel.

Many years later, King Saul was in a weak and desperate place, feeling very vulnerable as he sought and inquired of the Lord. His prayers were not being answered because he had forsaken God and was living in wicked, rebellious ways. God says that rebellion is as bad as witchcraft (see 1 Sam. 15:23), so it is not surprising that Saul's wickedness now caused him to seek out witchcraft that operated through a woman who had a familiar spirit.

> *And Saul disguised himself, and put on other raiment, and he went, and two men with him, and they came to the woman by night: and he said, I pray thee, divine unto me by the familiar spirit, and bring me him up, whom I shall name unto thee. And the woman said unto him, Behold, thou knowest what Saul hath done, how he hath cut off those that have familiar spirits, and the wizards, out of the land: wherefore then layest thou a snare for my life, to cause me to die? And Saul sware to her by the Lord, saying, As the Lord liveth, there shall no punishment happen to thee for this thing* (1 Samuel 28: 8-10).

Whatever word you want to use to describe her actions, the woman was receiving all her powers from a demonic source. It was witchcraft, and Saul sought to use it for counsel and guidance.

Satan has been using his seducing power to ensnare humankind ever since the Fall in the Garden of Eden. Today, the standoff is just as great between the genuine and the counterfeit.

Heavenly Father,

> *Please make me vulnerable to receive from You. Fill me with Your wisdom so I will not be deceived by anyone or anything. If there be any rebellion in me, please forgive me and keep me close to You. I thank You for Your promises to me. Help me place all my faith and trust in You and Your Word. Please guard me in the times of my life when I feel weak or desperate. I choose to fix my eyes on You, for You are the Author and the Finisher of my faith.*

In Your precious name, Amen.

MEDITATION SCRIPTURE

If any of you lacks wisdom, let him ask of God, who gives to all liberally and without reproach, and it will be given to him. But let him ask in faith, with no doubting, for he who doubts is like a wave of the sea driven and tossed by the wind. For let not that man suppose he will receive anything from the Lord; he is a double-minded man, unstable in all his ways (James 1:5-8 NKJV).

Devotional

Key Scriptures: 2 Timothy 1:7; Acts 19:13-16; Acts 19:11-12; Romans 14:17; John 8:44; Matthew 7:23; Matthew 7:15; Galatians 3:1; Matthew 24:24; Isaiah 8:19; 1 Samuel 8:6-9; 1 Samuel 15:23; 1 Samuel 28:8-10.

Key Point: Their outer appearance may not necessarily offend you—they may come in acceptable apparel and appealing mannerisms. This is why the Lord warns us to look inwardly at people's hearts, being sure to test the motives and ambitions that lie within them.

AN ENCOUNTER OF THE STRANGE KIND

1. What did the woman insistently and pointedly say?

_____

TWO DIFFERENT KINGDOMS

2. "I realized that I had stood against a _____ spirit."

3. *Webster's Dictionary* defines *deceived* as:
    a. To cause to believe an untruth
    b. To use or practice deceit
    c. Beguile
    d. Betray

    e. Delude

    f. Mislead

    g. All of the above

4. Living in a state of vulnerability is a bad thing. True or False?

5. "Some _____ or _____ operate with a deceitful supernatural power, while claiming to be _____."

BE ON GUARD

6. The Word says *false prophets* shall:

    a. Arise

    b. Possibly arise

    c. Flourish

    d. All of the above

7. In this Scripture, there is one tiny word that stands out above other words... "*For there shall arise false Christs, and false prophets, and shall show great signs and wonders; insomuch that, if it were possible they shall deceive the very elect*" (Matt. 24:24). Circle the "tiny word."

HOW QUICKLY WE FORGET

8. What brought the Hebrews out of slavery from the land of the Egyptians?

_____

_____

_____

9. Why were Saul's prayers not answered?

_____

_____

_____

CHAPTER 6

The Showdown

THE OPEN DOOR

It is important to recognize that demonic power is a very real counterfeit of the genuine power of God. It showed up when God was bringing His people out of Egypt by Moses' leadership.

When Moses first confronted Pharaoh, God allowed Pharaoh's power to be displayed alongside His. God always keeps things in and under His control. He chooses when, where, and how to display or prove His power is authentic. He's faithful to protect His people. His ultimate desire is that people recognize Him as the Lord. *"And the Egyptians shall know that I am the Lord, when I stretch out My hand on Egypt and bring out the children of Israel from among them"* (Exod. 7:5 NKJV). It is interesting to note, in Exodus 7:6, that Moses and Aaron did as the Lord commanded them. They were not operating out of rebellion or witchcraft, but were fully under direct orders and obeying the voice of the Lord their God.

ACTIONS SPEAK LOUDER THAN WORDS

Pharaoh's sorcerers and magicians were conjuring demons with enchantments and rituals. This is never a surprise to Heaven.

And the Lord spake unto Moses and unto Aaron, saying, "When Pharaoh shall speak unto you, saying, Show a miracle for you: then

57

thou shalt say unto Aaron, Take thy rod, and cast it before Pharaoh, and it shall become a serpent." And Moses and Aaron went in unto Pharaoh, and they did so as the Lord had commanded: and Aaron cast down his rod before Pharaoh, and before his servants, and it became a serpent. Then Pharaoh also called the wise men and the sorcerers: now the magicians of Egypt, they also did in like manner with their enchantments. For they cast down every man his rod, and they became serpents: but Aaron's rod swallowed up their rods (Exodus 7:8-12).

By lying signs and wonders the sorcerers and magicians were keeping people in bondage and fear. Their demonic assignment was to steal, kill, and destroy the Israelites. It should be very obvious why sin and rebellion open the door for witchcraft. Witchcraft searches for the agreement of sin. Sin is a "calling card" and open invitation for the demonic. In contrast, God searches for a pure heart and for a people willing and obedient to Him and His commandments. He yearns to lavish His love upon us and share His heart.

Pharaoh wanted to keep the people enslaved for his own personal gain, but God longs to have His people live the abundant life. The same controlling spirits of Egypt are in the world today. People may dress differently from ancient Egyptians; but whether in dirty, smelly rags, pressed classy expensive suits, or wearing long flowing robes—it makes no difference. Satan appears in many disguised forms through his demonic army and entices with many deceitful strategies. We must be sober-minded and spiritually alert to recognize the cunning and crafty tactics of our enemy. Ask yourself—Is the source of power from God or the demonic? This is why the Word says to "test the spirits."

How do you "test the spirits" of people? First of all, you will know them by their love; secondly, you will know them by their fruit; and thirdly, you will know them through the discernment of the Holy Spirit.

By this shall all men know that ye are my disciples, if ye have love one to another (John 13:35).

Ye shall know them by their fruits. Do men gather grapes of thorns, or figs of thistles? Even so every good tree bringeth forth good fruit; but a corrupt tree bringeth forth evil fruit. A good tree cannot bring forth evil fruit, neither can a corrupt tree bring forth good fruit. Every tree that bringeth not forth good fruit is hewn down, and cast into the fire. Wherefore by their fruits ye shall know them (Matthew 7:16-20).

God in His great wisdom and omniscience knew that Beelzebub, the "father of lies" or literally translated "lord of the flies," would lead the first rebellion and continue to operate through man's rebellion. Our great protection is to stay in submission to God's authority and obedience to His Word and will. His Word declares that obedience is better than sacrifice (see 1 Sam. 15:22). Why is it better? Obedience is an act of our will. Developing humility places us in a position of submission. *"Humble yourselves therefore under the mighty hand of God, that He may exalt you in due time"* (1 Peter 5:6). There is safety in submission to Him and those He has appointed over us. We need to be daily washed in the life-giving written Word. *"That He might sanctify and cleanse it* [the Church] *with the washing of water by the word, that He might present it to Himself a glorious Church, not having spot, or wrinkle, or any such thing; but that it should be holy and without blemish"* (Eph. 5:26-27). We must each submit to the Lordship of Jesus Christ and embrace the crucified way of life. *"And He said to them all, If any man will come after Me, let him deny himself, and take up his cross daily, and follow Me"* (Luke 9:23). We must appropriate the redemptive work of His shed blood on Calvary.

One day in prayer I asked the Lord, "How do I stay humble?" Even as I said it, fear tugged at my heart, for this is a risky question. I was bracing myself, ready to be humiliated in front of a group of people in order to "practice" humility. To "practice" humility implies I was not ready to grasp humility as the very fabric of my being, but only as a momentary experience to impress others and God. Actually, this can be a form of self-abasement, for I was thinking that if I devalued myself I would become humble. This "practice" can bolster a poor self-image, which may appear as humility, but is in reality false humility. This is not His view of humility. God was showing me the great value He had placed upon me, which would result in true humility and give me a grateful heart.

His ways are not our ways...they are much, much higher! His reply to me that day surprised me. He said, "It is hard to become proud if you remain at the foot of My cross keeping your eyes fixed on My face—your eyes gazing into My eyes—as I paid the price for you on Calvary." I began to visualize what He meant. I was reminded of what Isaiah prophesied:

> *He is despised and rejected of men; a man of sorrows, and acquainted with grief: and we hid as it were our faces from Him; He was despised, and we esteemed Him not. Surely He hath borne our griefs, and carried our sorrows: yet we did esteem Him stricken, smitten of God, and afflicted. But He was wounded for our transgressions, He was bruised for our iniquities: the chastisement of our peace was upon Him; and with His stripes we are healed* (Isaiah 53:3-5).

He alone paid the price for all of us and He alone deserves all glory and all praise! It is a privilege and honor to give back to Him His own glory. We need to live a life of absolute abandonment and surrender under His love, care, and Lordship. According to *Webster's Dictionary*, the word *humble* refers to someone who is meek, modest, or lowly of mind. The goal of true humility is to believe God will use us and move through us, in spite of ourselves. False humility entraps and causes us to think we are worthless, that God cannot possibly use us for His glory. We must embrace His example of true humility and always be available to declare with boldness His wonders upon the face of the earth.

> *Let this mind be in you, which was also in Christ Jesus: who, being in the form of God, thought it not robbery to be equal with God: but made Himself of no reputation, and took upon Him the*

form of a servant, and was made in the likeness of men: and being found in fashion as a man, He humbled Himself, and became obedient unto death, even the death of the cross (Philippians 2:5-8).

EYES OF THE HOLY SPIRIT

As I explained in my book, *Embraced by the Holy Spirit*, the Holy Spirit is our teacher who leads, directs, guides, and keeps us in truth. We must remain in a position of humility, in order to be taught and led by Him. Our traveling clothes should include the cloak of humility and a backpack. In this backpack are the gifts of the Holy Spirit, including the gift of discernment of spirits. The word *discern* is a verb, an action word that means "to detect with the eyes or distinguish." This means we are to use the eyes of the Holy Spirit to recognize what we are sensing, feeling, and seeing. To be discerning is to gain insight and understanding. We must always remember it is important we fully embrace God's written Word. The occult or witchcraft sometimes will take a portion of God's Word and twist it as a way to entice you. This is why it is imperative to always be led by the Holy Spirit in giving a word, as well as receiving a word.

Jesus instructed us to be led by His Holy Spirit. "*For as many as are led by the Spirit of God, they are the sons of God*" (Rom. 8:14). We must be led in our pursuit of a prophetic word, as well as in giving a prophetic word. I receive thousands and thousands of requests from people who claim God told them, "Eileen, you have a word for me." We should all desire prophetic words from one of God's mouthpieces, so I totally understand the need, want, and desire. However, many times this is our soul man reaching out to grab from another Spirit-led human vessel, rather than seeking the Lord for ourselves. Doing this can open the door to receive a soulish response. When flesh solicits flesh, it produces a fleshly response. How do I know this? I have done it myself and would like to share one of my experiences.

SURPRISE, SURPRISE

This personal experience happened over 20 years ago. My husband, Fred, was in the Army and we were stationed in Germany. Our time of departure was approaching, and I was seeking guidance from the Lord as to what He would have me do during our next duty assignment. So, I went off to a conference in Germany where there were awesome prophetic speakers ministering and flowing in the Spirit of the Lord.

I had decided that *I* would go up and *I* would get a word from the Lord through a particular person. As the man was ministering, he loudly spoke into the microphone, "I know just what you need, sister." I smiled, happy that God was about to speak to me. Boy, was I in for a surprise! Here I stood, surrounded by a thousand people. In fact, I had prayed with and prophesied over some of them the day prior. They, too, were eager to hear what God was about to speak over me.

The minister loudly and boldly proclaimed, "You need the Baptism of the Holy Spirit and your heavenly prayer language." Full of embarrassment and confusion, I thought I would save face by praying in tongues. Little did I know God was answering my prayer for more humility! A roaring response came forth as the people in the conference clapped their hands and cheered Heaven, thinking I had just received a brand-new heavenly language and the Baptism of the Holy Spirit. (By the way, the applause was a little late—I had received the Baptism five years prior!) To say I was dumbfounded is to underestimate my reaction.

In my desperation, I found the closest exit and fled to my room. With boldness and humiliation I loudly cried out to God, "What was *that* all about?" His reply to me was, "You sought a word in the soulish realm, and I gave you a word in the soulish realm. I want you to learn to be led by My Holy Spirit in giving words as well as receiving My words." It was a humiliating, life-changing, and extremely uncomfortable lesson. After eating my humble pie, I was much wiser, knowing that the "flesh profits nothing." I did not cherish the thought of having to leave my room and face the other people. Believe me, it is far more comfortable to be corrected and taught in private than to be groomed and trained in public. I promise you, the school of humility is still very much in existence today. I caution you to heed the wisdom I have gleaned from my own experience. It is God's highest desire that we always be led and directed by the Spirit of the Lord. This is part of being trained in our daily lives through the gifts of the Spirit and through the presence of God Almighty.

Moses was much wiser than many of us. He said, *"If Your Presence does not go with us, do not bring us up from here"* (Exod. 33:15 NKJV). Moses was about to stand against the powers of darkness and he needed God's presence to combat the Egyptians in order to win. Moses won and the people were brought out to their freedom because of the manifest presence of God. If Moses needed the presence of God in his day, how much more do we need it today?

Heavenly Father,

Help me to know You as the Great "I AM." Show me all my sins, both known and unknown. I renounce all agreement that I or those I love have made with the demonic. If there be any open door for demonic activity to enter in, I close it off now and seal it with the precious blood of Jesus. If the enemy is using tactics against me or those I love, please show me how to overcome him. I humble myself under Your hand for You to correct those You love. Please call me into a greater intimacy with You and remind me to stay and always be aware of Your presence. I do hunger and thirst after You.

In the name of Jesus, Amen.

MEDITATION SCRIPTURE

And He said unto them, Go ye into all the world, and preach the gospel to every creature. He that believeth and is baptized shall be saved; but he that believeth not shall be damned. And these signs shall follow them that believe; in My name shall they cast out devils; they shall speak with new tongues; they shall take up serpents; and if they drink any deadly thing, it shall not hurt them; they shall lay hands on the sick, and they shall recover. So then after the Lord had spoken unto them, He was received up into heaven, and sat on the right hand of God. And they went forth, and preached every where, the Lord working with them, and confirming the word with signs following. Amen (Mark 16:15-20).

Devotional

Key Scriptures: Exodus 7:5-12; John 13:35; Matthew 7:16-20; 1 Samuel 15:22; 1 Peter 5:6; Ephesians 5:26-27; Luke 9:23; Isaiah 53:3-5; Philippians 2:5-8; Romans 8:14; Exodus 33:15.

Key Point: We need to live a life of absolute abandonment and surrender under His love, care, and Lordship. True humility is to believe God will use us and move through us, in spite of ourselves. False humility entraps and causes us to think we are worthless; that God cannot possibly use us for His glory.

THE OPEN DOOR

1. "His ultimate desire is that _____."

ACTIONS SPEAK LOUDER THAN WORDS

2. "_____ searches for the agreement of sin."

3. How do you test the spirits?

_____

_____

_____

4. Keeping your eyes on His cross and fixing your eyes on the face of Jesus; realizing the price paid for you on Calvary—what will this realization create in you?

EYES OF THE HOLY SPIRIT

5. What's in our "backpack"?

_____

_____

_____

6. *Discern* means to:
   a. Guess
   b. Describe
   c. Detect
   d. All of the above
7. Is it imperative to be led by the Holy Spirit in both giving a word and receiving a word? Yes or No (Circle one.)

SURPRISE, SURPRISE

8. "_____ had decided that _____ would go up and _____ would get a word from the Lord through this person."
9. If you seek a word in the soulish realm, what will you get? Have you ever fallen into this trap and how did you respond?

_____

_____

_____

CHAPTER 7

Prophetic Interference

THE SHIFT

The fear of the Lord must rule and reign in our lives. It will help guard us from sin and protect us from living in habitual sin, which will eventually destroy us. Years ago, I knew of a sweet couple in their mid-thirties, both of whom appeared very loving and kind. They were caught in error because of their immaturity in the ways of the Lord. Because the man was living a double lifestyle, his rebellion left the door open to severe deception.

This couple chased after people who would prophesy into their lives, and I happened to be one of those people. At the time, I was also young in the ways of the Lord and susceptible to flattery, which caused me to operate in counterfeit mercy. This means pitying people and feeding their self-pity, instead of empathizing with them. Counterfeit mercy keeps their souls crippled and unable to mature and grow. Jesus never operated in counterfeit mercy, but was full of true compassion and mercy. *"And Jesus went forth, and saw a great multitude, and was moved with compassion toward them, and He healed their sick"* (Matt. 14:14).

This couple always seemed to be depressed and wanting to know God's will, but they never seemed to find it. It seemed easier for them to call me every week for a prophetic word. Because I felt sorry for them, I would pray and say, "The Lord says." This went on for about five weeks. One morning in my private prayer time, the Lord convicted me and said, "You are leading these people to depend upon you instead of Me." (Ouch!)

He said, "When they call again you are to reply, 'The Lord has been missing your voice and longs to speak to you Himself.'"

My responsibility was to shift their eyes from me to Him and in the process, let the Holy Spirit work with His power of conviction. In no uncertain terms, He let me know that I was not their Savior or Lord.

I love prophecies and I love to prophesy. I rejoice hearing reports of the awesome fruit in the lives of God's precious people. But if you were to ask me to choose between prophecy and my intimate walk with the Lord, there would be no choice. Intimacy with the Lord must always, always supercede all of the gifts of the Holy Spirit. Yet, we must also honor and respect the gifts, because they are God given. "*Follow after charity* [love], *and desire spiritual gifts, but rather that ye may prophesy*" (1 Cor. 14:1). Through fellowship and cultivating an intimate relationship with the Lord, you will be able to quickly and accurately discern and detect the spirits that are around you. This is why God in His wisdom gave us the first commandment: "*I am the Lord your God...you shall have no other gods before Me*" (Exod. 20:2-3 NKJV).

It is wonderful that our Father gave us His only Son, Jesus. He gives us above and beyond all that we can ever ask, think, or imagine. Jesus said that when we ask for the Holy Spirit, He will certainly give us the Spirit.

> *If a son asks for bread from any father among you, will he give him a stone? Or if he asks for a fish, will he give him a serpent instead of a fish? Or if he asks for an egg, will he offer him a scorpion? If you then, being evil, know how to give good gifts to your children, how much more will your heavenly Father give the Holy Spirit to those who ask Him!* (Luke 11:11-13 NKJV)

When the Holy Spirit came, He brought with Him gifts for all of us to use. God longs for us to grow up, and become reflectors of His Son. Jesus not only prophesied—He had discernment; He healed; He did signs, wonders, and miracles; He exercised every gift of the Holy Spirit. *"Now to Him who is able to do exceedingly abundantly above all that we ask or think, according to the power that works in us, to Him be glory in the church by Christ Jesus to all generations, forever and ever. Amen"* (Eph. 3:20-21 NKJV).

No Substitute Here

Religion sometimes says, "Give us a king or a leader." Religion tries to substitute by giving us a man, whom we want to be God in the flesh—much like the Israelites did when they pushed God away and demanded a king. Dead religion does not recognize the voice or move of the Holy Spirit. Why not? Because death cannot respond or acknowledge the beckoning of the Holy Spirit. Death leads to decay. In contrast, Jesus is alive and offers life.

This is why many of the Pharisees did not recognize Jesus as the Messiah. They were "dead men walking." *"Woe unto you, scribes and Pharisees, hypocrites! for ye are like unto whited sepulchres, which indeed appear beautiful outward, but are within full of dead men's bones, and of all uncleanness"* (Matt. 23:27).

I recall a time when I was invited to minister at a Sunday evening service in a Midwest church. I was about to step into an extremely sorrowful situation. This dear pastor was a tall, white-haired man with dull looking eyes full of discouragement and pain. He walked with a limp and his shoulders stooped over, which gave him an appearance of having been severely beaten down. After he introduced me, I glanced in his direction and saw he was very guarded. He rigidly sat straight up, making me feel quite intimidated.

Apathetically he said, "Show me your stuff."

The atmosphere was unwelcoming, and there was minimal liberty or agreement. I knew the Holy Spirit was grieving, and I sensed His decision: "We don't have to." In my heart, I replied, "Uh oh, what do You want to do?"

The lukewarmness of the church felt like it must match the temperature of the poor man's heart. The service was cold and extremely short.

I wish I could say it was a short but sweet service, but this was not so. It was extraordinarily sad; I prayed for only four or five people because of the pervasive apathy.

When I asked the Holy Spirit what had happened, He replied, "He [the pastor] has set himself in extreme judgment. He has not only closed himself in, but has also closed others out, including Me and My gifts."

I felt the disappointment and sorrow of my friend the Holy Spirit. Neither of us had felt loved or welcomed in that service. The Holy Spirit came in tongues of fire to brighten up everyone and everything; yet, sadly, it was obvious that there had been no fire in this house of the Lord for a multitude of years. Looking around the room, I saw very few bright eyes that reflected the light of the Spirit. It was all very heart-breaking.

The Holy Spirit wants to be longed for, and He wants people to reach out for the warmth and comfort of His presence. If you would like to learn more about intimacy with the Holy Spirit, I encourage you to read *Embraced by the Holy Spirit*. Perhaps because of circumstances and pain, some are gripped and paralyzed, unable to cry out. You only need to ask Him to pour out the fire of His presence on your cold heart and into a cold situation. If you desire to keep your motives and your heart pure, He will respond! He is looking for hearts that are open to be healed and restored, so Jesus alone may be glorified. "*Blessed are the pure in heart: for they shall see God*" (Matt. 5:8).

Do You Get the Yoke?

God has a wonderful sense of humor. In fact, He is the Creator of all righteous humor and holds the patent for having the most profound sense of humor in the whole universe.

I knew back in that church sat a pastor who needed to have the precious fellowship and laughter that comes from the heart of God. Unfortunately, he had closed the door. The Lord desires to share joy and laughter with His people, even if they are unwilling to receive it. "*He will yet fill your mouth with laughing, and your lips with rejoicing*" (Job 8:21 NKJV).

One morning at home, I had just barely opened my eyes when I heard the Father say, "All three of Us are in love with you." I felt my face begin to blush with embarrassment. I knew that God loved me, but for Him to declare He was *in love* with me, as well as the Holy Spirit and Jesus, was stretching me into a deeper, more intimate level of faith. I heard Him repeat, "All three of Us are in love with you." With His second declaration of love, my embarrassment only grew. I smiled to myself and began to laugh. I replied back, "I am in love with all three of You, too." I thought this would be the end of the conversation, so I changed the subject and went about starting to cook breakfast, which is usually one egg and toast. When I cracked the egg shell open, out popped three bright yellow yolks! I was speechless as I stared in the pan. I knew this was more than a coincidence...it was a God incident. I knew God was still speaking to me and again I heard Him say, "All three of Us are in love with you and that is no yolk!" I have never had another egg like that, but I still smile and laugh, as I also declare to you, "All three of Them are in love with you, too, and that's no yoke."

Heavenly Father,

Forgive me for the times I have been judgmental or critical of others or tried to be their savior and lord. Remind me that Jesus alone is Lord, and help me convey that to others. Please make me aware of the times I have grieved and hurt the Holy Spirit. I have the sincere desire to never quench Him, yet I know I have at times. Please, Holy Spirit, forgive me for my presumption and self-righteousness. Father, help me obey You and Your Word, so I might wholly follow the Holy Spirit and declare that Jesus alone is Lord of all.

In Your glorious name, Amen.

MEDITATION SCRIPTURE:

Rejoice evermore. Pray without ceasing. In every thing give thanks: for this is the will of God in Christ Jesus concerning you.

Quench not the Spirit. Despise not prophesyings. Prove all things; hold fast that which is good. Abstain from all appearance of evil. And the very God of peace sanctify you wholly; and I pray God your whole spirit and soul and body be preserved blameless unto the coming of our Lord Jesus Christ. Faithful is he that calleth you, who also will do it (1 Thessalonians 5:16-24).

ℰ𝒆𝑜𝑜𝑡𝑖𝑜𝑛𝑎𝑙

Key Scriptures: Matthew 14:14; 1 Corinthians 14:1; Exodus 20:2-3; Luke 11:11-13; Ephesians 3:20-21; Matthew 23:27; Matthew 5:8; Job 8:21.

Key Point: Intimacy with the Lord must always, always supercede all of the gifts of the Holy Spirit. Yet, we must also honor and respect the gifts. Through fellowship by cultivating an intimate relationship with the Lord, you will be able to quickly and accurately discern and detect the spirits that are around you.

THE SHIFT

1. What helps guard us from sin and protects us from living a sinful life that can eventually destroy us?

_____

_____

_____

2. "You are leading these people to depend upon _____ and not upon _____."

No Substitute Here

3. Dead religion does not recognize the voice or move of the Holy Spirit. Why not?

_____

_____

_____

Do You Get the Yoke?

4. "*He will fill your mouth with* _____ *and your lips* _____"
   (Job 8:21 NKJV).

5. How many yolks were in the egg?
   a. Twenty
   b. Two
   c Three
   d. None of the above
   e. This is just a "yoke" question

CHAPTER 8

Integrity of the Prophetic

IN THE FULLNESS OF TIME

Integrity is crucial in living the life God has called us to live; in fact, it is a requirement for flowing in the prophetic. God is concerned about heart and integrity issues, just as He is concerned about the accuracy of a prophetic word. We all bear the responsibility of bringing forth the highest word from the throne room of God. *Strong's Concordance* defines *integrity* as "uprightness, innocence, completeness and simplicity." "*Let integrity and uprightness preserve me; for I wait on Thee*" (Ps. 25:21).

One of the greatest pitfalls of the prophetic is people who become angry, unteachable, or offended, and who defend themselves rather than standing behind the Word of the Lord. They want to protect their image and pride. Few of us would choose the walk of Old Testament prophets like Ezekiel, who was known for illustrated sermons to make a point well understood by the hearers. God called him not only to prophesy, but to act out the prophetic word.

> *Now the word of the Lord came to me, saying "Son of man, you dwell in the midst of a rebellious house, which has eyes to see but does not see, and ears to hear but does not hear, for they are a rebellious house. Therefore, son of man, prepare your belongings for captivity, and go into captivity by day in their sight. You shall go from your*

place into captivity to another place in their sight. It may be that they will consider, though they are a rebellious house. By day you shall bring out your belongings in their sight, as though going into captivity; and at evening you shall go in their sight, like those who go into captivity. Dig through the wall in their sight, and carry your belongings out through it. In their sight, you shall bear them on your shoulders and carry them out at twilight; you shall cover your face so that you cannot see the ground, for I have made you a sign to the house of Israel." So I did as I was commanded (Ezekiel 12:1-7a NKJV).

Think about this…Ezekiel was a prophet of integrity who was willing to lose his dignity, his pride, and his privacy. Consequently, he was willing to be labeled strange and weird in order to drive God's messages home. No wonder Ezekiel's name means "God strengthens"—he certainly needed God's strength!

It appears that prophetic people today quickly and easily let words roll off their tongues. They may wound the hearts of people and never look back, take responsibility, or try to bring "damage control." As a result of a lack of integrity, many ministries spend time breaking off false prophecies and soulish prophecies. Plus, they must deal with the pain, disappointment, and rejection these prophecies have deposited in the hearts and spirits of innocent listeners.

I know some people think that when you deliver a prophecy, you should never look back; yet, one of the greatest tests of a true prophecy is whether it has been fulfilled. By withholding his agreement, the prophet Jeremiah took a stand against false prophets who prophesied peace for Israel and Judah, when God had decreed war and judgment. It's interesting to note the small word *grit* in *integrity*. Jeremiah needed "true grit" in order to stand strong and bring forth only the word of the Lord. "*As for the prophet who prophesies of peace, when the word of the prophet comes to pass, the prophet will be known as one whom the Lord has truly sent*" (Jer. 28:9 NKJV). So to look back, is to know that a prophet of the Lord has been sent. What God has said will happen, does indeed happen.

This is a great way to test prophecy, but it will not work in all cases. There is another element that is involved in the prophetic—God's timing. Many times in Scripture the phrase "In the fullness of time" is used, with good reason. Although Isaiah prophesied the birth, life, and death of Jesus, he never lived to see the fulfillment. By being the declarative voice of the Lord, He was used by God to establish the coming of the Messiah to earth. Throughout the ages, God has also allowed other prophets to catch a glimpse of God's eternal plan, which continues to unfold.

> *Of which salvation the **prophets** have inquired and searched diligently, who **prophesied** of the grace that should come unto you: searching what, or what **manner of time** the Spirit of Christ which was in them did signify, when it testified beforehand the sufferings of Christ, and the glory that should follow. Unto whom it was revealed, that not unto themselves, but unto us they did minister the things, which are now reported unto you by them that have preached the gospel unto you with the Holy Ghost sent down from heaven; which things the angels desire to look into* (1 Peter 1:1-12).

HIS LOYAL SERVANTS

"Surely the Lord God does nothing, unless He reveals His secret to His servants the prophets" (Amos 3:7 NKJV). You may think that the pivotal word in this Scripture is *secret* or *reveals*, but I think the word is *servants*. A servant must have "inside information" in order to serve his Master at the highest level. It is one thing to have revelation, and it is something else to carry a secret; but both of those may be hidden in your heart. Having these private insights can also be a handicap and hindrance for you, because they are sacred and are between you and the Master. Your motivation for where and when to share them must stay pure. Treasure and honor these insights, but keep them in their rightful place, and guard your heart against self-importance.

A true servant wants to protect the deepest, most intimate secrets between himself and the Master. However, releasing revelation to bene-fit Him is by far a greater gift of love to the Lord and to those He loves. To share something publicly and still bring honor and glory to the Master, is to demonstrate that you are His loyal servant. A good test is to ask yourself: "Will my speaking benefit God's Kingdom and another person, or my own agenda?"

Years ago, God spoke to me the term "spiritual rape." In the prophetic position, God will give you personal details and insights into the lives of others, in order to bring hope and healing. We must use dis-cernment. Sometimes it's something God wants you to only pray about. Other times it's to be shared with that person. In that case, these intimate insights must remain confidential between you and the other person. To tattle or recklessly repeat the insights the Lord has given you causes a "raping" of this person's soul. What you are doing is literally exposing or uncovering them. God grieves deeply when this is done, because you have taken upon yourself to strip off the very robe of right-eousness He placed over that person. You are inviting others to join you in a "spiritual rape." This is a graphic illustration, but a necessary one. We must clearly understand the seriousness of integrity with Almighty God.

To be identified with the Master, it is important to always remember whom you represent when you are sharing any of His revelations with His people. Whatever you, a servant, do will reflect on the name of your Master, by bringing Him either glory or dishonor. Speaking for God must be accepted as an extremely grave responsibility. *"Therefore, whether you eat or drink, or whatever you do, do all to the glory of God"* (1Cor. 10:31 NKJV).

THE POWER OF CHOICE

A problem will arise when we have impure motives or hidden selfish ambitions. Although we may cover it well in front of others, our God in Heaven reads the hearts of His people. *But the Lord said to Samuel, "Do not look at his appearance or at his physical stature, because I have refused him. For the Lord does not see as man sees; for man looks at the outward appearance, but the Lord looks at the heart"* (1 Sam. 16:7 NKJV).

God is not impressed with those who speak forth things in His name, yet live one way in public and another way in private. God warns many times in private; but if they do not heed the warning, eventually the sin will be exposed in public. We are warned not to live double-minded or dishonest, deceitful lifestyles. This dishonors the Lord and brings disgrace to the Body of Christ. It is not God's will or His best, because it gives a foothold for a spirit of rebellion to take root and opens the door for the demonic. Remember, a spirit of rebellion breeds witch-craft, which always strives to shut down the true prophetic.

"Observe and obey all these words which I command you, that it may go well with you and your children after you forever, when you do what is good and right in the sight of the Lord your God" (Deut. 12:28 NKJV). God is a God who sees behind closed doors; with Him, there are no secrets. *"For there is nothing covered, that shall not be revealed; neither hid, that shall not be known. Therefore whatsoever ye have spoken in darkness shall be heard in the light; and that which ye have spoken in the ear in closets shall be proclaimed upon the housetops"* (Luke 12:2-3).

Just as good things are shared in secret, so can deceptive ideas be birthed in secret. Then the door is opened for an unholy agreement, an ungodly alliance. When this happens, we invite the spirit of enticement. As shared earlier in Chapter 5, enticing someone brings them into deception by compromising and twisting the Word of God to fit their own hidden agenda—as was the case with the New Age woman's words. In turn, they draw others to join them in living a "lie of compromise." True prophets always draw people closer to the will, desire, and ways of God without compromise. False prophets lead people astray to follow after themselves or some unacceptable lifestyle, contrary to God and His Word.

While the true prophetic person declares God's highest desire, he or she must honor the free will of the listeners, whether an individual or a nation—because God Himself does. The one prophesied to may abort

God's plans by making choices contrary to His will and His prophetic word.

> *The kingdom of heaven is like unto a certain king, which made a marriage for his son, and sent forth his servants to call them that were bidden to the wedding: and they would not come. Again, he sent forth other servants, saying, Tell them which are bidden, Behold, I have prepared my dinner: my oxen and my fatlings are killed, and all things are ready: come unto the marriage. But they made light of it, and went their ways, one to his farm, another to his merchandise* (Matthew 22:2-5).

OBEY HIS VOICE

Satan comes as an "angel of light" to capture you by a counterfeit sign or wonder and to encourage you to chase after false gods—whether money, position, flattery, power, or self-idolatry. False prophets or people of enticement, drawing from their demonic power, will speak a dream or flattering word that can "puff you up." We are warned to turn away from such people and to give our allegiance to God alone:

> *If there arises among you a prophet or a dreamer of dreams, and he gives you a sign or a wonder, and the sign or the wonder comes to pass, of which he spoke to you, saying, "Let us go after other gods"—which you have not known—"and let us serve them," you shall not listen to the words of that prophet or that dreamer of dreams, for the Lord your God is testing you to know whether you love the Lord your God with all your heart and with all your soul. You shall walk after the Lord your God and fear Him, and keep His commandments and obey His voice; you shall serve Him and hold fast to Him* (Deuteronomy 13:1-4 NKJV).

We must go back and understand what is stated here. There will be an uprising of false prophets, dreamers and those who will bring forth counterfeit wonders, whether it is through divination, witchcraft, a familiar spirit or a seducing spirit. They all come with the same goal; to lead you into rebellion and to have you usurp the authority of God and His Word. Believe me when I tell you, the enemy is fighting to block the will of God in your life. He wants to rob your destiny by influencing your free will and agreement to build his rebellious kingdom.

There is only one safeguard against this and that is obeying His commandments. In doing so, there is protection and security. God always watches over His own Word and those who keep His Word written in their hearts.

UNDERMINING GOD'S PLAN

I remember a situation where it was very clear God's will and authority were not being accomplished. Whether or not the person involved was aware of what was happening, observers could see that enticing and seducing spirits were at work. This woman was being driven by an unholy love and longing for position and power. She began to court others with flattery and subtle compliments, in order to make herself indispensable. *"And such as do wickedly against the covenant shall he corrupt by flatteries: but the people that do know their God shall be strong, and do exploits"* (Dan. 11:32).

Learning that a statewide organization had an open board position, this woman immediately coveted it. Because of bylaws and the logistics of the organization, specific guidelines had to be followed in filling the position. I was contacted, along with two others from different parts of the state, to pray and seek the Lord as to whom He would have serve. None of us knew each other personally, but we decided via phone that we would all fast for three days and afterward meet in a common city. Together, we would meet with a selection committee chairman and submit the name we had each separately received in our private prayer time. The date was decided, and we began our fasts.

After meeting and greeting each other in a friendly manner, we proceeded to a small conference room. We each wrote a name on a slip of paper and placed it on the table upside down. Hungry and in a hurry, I waited with anticipation and excitement for the reading of the names. In prayer, I had clearly heard the name I was given and why this person was chosen. The chairperson began to read the names. The first name, the second name, and the third name were read. None of us were surprised, for we all had received the same name. We were confident we had heard the voice of the Lord.

Then a strange and peculiar look crossed the face of the chairperson. She smugly thanked us for our time and prayers. We were quite startled by what happened next.

The chairperson abruptly stood up, pushed back her chair, and said, "I prayed, too, and God told me that I was to fill the position." We looked at each other in disbelief. We knew she had schemed and maneuvered, placing her will above God's. By questioning, we tried to understand her reasoning and motive. It was like talking to a wall, because she was determined to exert herself. Feeling like abused puppets, we finally left for lunch, knowing that she had patronized us by allowing us to go through the motions. We felt powerless and ineffective.

I am sorry to say, the organization went downhill after that situation. God was no longer in control because a person's will had pushed through her own plan. Three years later, I was once again invited to be a part of the election team. Excusing myself, and with a taint of sarcasm in my voice, I replied, "I don't miss food three days for nothing," and we all laughed. We had watched firsthand a seductive spirit accomplish what it had been sent to do.

We must all guard ourselves and stay in a position of humility; seeking first the Kingdom of God. It is more important to look for the one who carries the anointing, than for the one who carries man's popular vote. "*Let nothing be done through strife or vainglory; but in lowliness of mind let each esteem other*[s] *better than themselves*" (Phil. 2:3).

Heavenly Father,

Create a heart in me that will be able to treasure and carry Your secrets. Prepare me to be one of Your trustworthy vessels. Keep me teachable and help me not to be easily offended. Do not let me be held back or controlled by what people do or don't do. Let me always be mindful that this is not about me, but Jesus. Thank you for Your life, death, and resurrection. Thank You, Jesus, for all You have done for me. Father, place me in Your timeline for things to happen in my life. Help me not to fight Your timing, but to trust You every minute and hour with my life. Keep me seeking Your Kingdom and righteousness. Help me know my days are held in Your hand.

In Jesus' precious name, Amen.

MEDITATION

Who is the man [or woman] that fears the Lord? _____ [your name] shall He teach in the way He chooses. _____ himself [/herself] shall dwell in prosperity, and _____'s descendants shall inherit the earth. The secret of the Lord is with those who fear Him, and He will show _____ His covenant (Psalm 25:12-14 NKJV).

MEDITATION SCRIPTURE

But seek ye first the kingdom of God, and His righteousness; and all these things shall be added unto you. Take therefore no thought for the morrow: for the morrow shall take thought for the things of itself. Sufficient unto the day is the evil thereof (Matthew 6:33-34).

Devotional

Key Scriptures: Psalm 25:21; Ezekiel 12:1-7a; Jeremiah 28:9; 1 Peter 1:1-12; Amos 3:7; 1 Corinthians 10:31; 1 Samuel 16:7; Deuteronomy 12:28; Luke 12:2-3; Matthew 22:2-5; Deuteronomy 13:1-4; Daniel 11:32; Philippians 2:3.

Key Point: God is not impressed with those who speak forth things in His name, yet live one way in public and another way in private.

IN THE FULLNESS OF TIME

1. "One of the greatest pitfalls of the prophetic is people who become
_____, _____, or _____, and who defend themselves rather than _____."

2. "*As for the prophet who prophesies of peace, when the word of the prophet comes to pass, the prophet will be known as one whom the Lord has truly sent.*" True or False?

3. Many times in Scripture, the phrase "In the fullness of time" is used. What's the reason for this term?

_____

_____

_____

HIS LOYAL SERVANTS

4. God loves to share secrets. True or False? What Scripture backs up your answer?

_____

_____

THE POWER OF CHOICE

5. What are the results of deceptive ideas birthed in secret?

_____

_____

_____

6. True prophets always draw people closer to the will, desire, and ways of God without compromise. This is the case:
   a. Usually
   b. Always
   c. Conditionally
   d. None of the above

OBEY HIS VOICE

7. "Believe me when I tell you, the enemy is fighting to block the will of God in your life. He wants to rob your destiny by influencing your _____ and _____ to _____."

UNDERMINING GOD'S PLAN

8. Is it more important to look for <u>the one who carries the anointing</u> *or* <u>the one who carries man's popular vote?</u> (Circle one.)

CHAPTER 9

How to Hear

DRAW FROM THE WELL

After reading the story in the previous chapter, you may be asking how you can be sure you are hearing the voice of the Lord—not a seducing spirit or your own thoughts? This is a very common and important question. I will try to explain from my limited understanding, but through my full range of experience. In Chapter 1, I related how I naively asked the question, "What's a prophecy?" Here I want to help clarify how we receive, respond to, and flow in the prophetic. The Holy Spirit wants to teach and train us all to grow in maturity in the gifts. "*Now concerning spiritual gifts, brethren, I would not have you ignorant*" (1 Cor. 12:1).

God has given each one of us a spirit which becomes a "well" of salvation after we are born again. God is Spirit. God will speak and place in our spirit (or "well") His thoughts, His words, His visions, His dreams. At the appointed time, He will release them under the anointing of the Holy Spirit. "*But ye have an unction from the Holy One, and ye know all things*" (1 John 2:20).

I want to give you a picture of a well, a very, very deep well filled with living water, but also filled with great treasures—His diamonds, His rubies, His gold, and His silver. Precious treasures! "*But we have this treasure in earthen vessels, that the excellency of the power may be of God, and not of us*" (2 Cor. 4:7).

At the top of this well is a bucket to which is attached a red scarlet rope. An all-wise and all-knowing Person is in control of lowering and raising the bucket. He knows where each and every precious gift or stone is deposited. How? Because He is has made the deposit. This Person is the Spirit of the Lord, and *the well is your spirit*. The anointing is the unction that draws the water out of your well. Because the red rope is the blood of Jesus and has access to your well, you can follow His voice and fellowship with His Spirit to declare the Kingdom of God on earth through heavenly gifts. If you feel a tugging on the rope, what does this mean? It is the unction or anointing of the Holy Spirit drawing from your spirit. This is the Lord's way of letting you know He wants to make a withdrawal from your bucket to build up the Body of Christ. "*He that believeth on me, as the scripture hath said, out of his belly shall flow rivers of living water*" (John 7:38).

You may experience a prompting, a tugging, or a very strong impression from His Spirit—a Holy Ghost "heads up." Sometimes He seems like a gentle tap on the shoulder. Because you are familiar with Him, you can sense and recognize His presence. The Book of Acts describes the Holy Spirit's coming with a recognizable and tangible power; and as far as I know, He has not left yet! When He first arrived on the scene, the waiting worshipers all became filled with the Spirit and full of the "new wine."

> *For these are not drunken, as ye suppose, seeing it is but the third hour of the day. But this is that which was spoken by the prophet Joel; And it shall come to pass in the last days, saith God, I will pour out of My Spirit upon all flesh: and your sons and your daughters shall prophesy, and your young men shall see visions, and your old men shall dream dreams. And on My servants and on My handmaidens I will pour out in those days of My Spirit, and they shall prophesy* (Acts 2:15-18).

Today, He will nudge you with the same power of His presence, and it will feel as though someone is applying pressure on you to get your attention. He will continue to apply pressure, making you aware that He wants to do something with you or with someone else. Therefore, you are led by the power and the impression of the Holy Spirit. He, this Wonderful Person, is an invisible force who impresses your spirit over and over again.

KNOW HIS DRAWING

God draws the prophetic out of us to build His Body and to make declarations of His Kingdom on earth. When you minister in the prophetic, you will feel the drawing of the Holy Spirit toward a certain person, just like a "bee is drawn to honey." The anointing within you is being drawn upon, the gift is being pulled on, and you are connected with and impressed upon by the Spirit of God. Within your spirit you know when His prophetic word goes to this person or that person, because the Holy Spirit has given you the spirit of enlightenment.

It is crucial to be attentive and not allow yourself to be distracted by outer surroundings or by the pressure of people. Stay sensitive to the pulling of the Holy Spirit. Use extreme, utmost discipline to block out all distractions around you. This clears the path for the pouring out of the Holy Spirit on an individual or a group. "*And when he putteth forth his own sheep, he goeth before them, and the sheep follow him: for they know his voice*" (John 10:4). I want to share an example of a mistake I made about 20 years ago. (Please give me grace in my moment of truth!)

STAY FOCUSED

I was in a church praying with people, and a long line had formed waiting for me to prophesy. I had entered into the flow of the Holy Spirit and was moving along quickly, smoothly, and effectively. I was following the Holy Spirit's instructions, as well as releasing the words He was impressing upon me to declare into each person's life. All was well. The background music was appropriate, people's hearts were open, and I was hearing the Lord loud and clear for each and every individual.

All of a sudden, out of nowhere, I felt a tugging on my right arm, and on my left shoulder I felt the weight of someone who obviously wanted my undivided attention. At first, I was bewildered and confused.

I thought to myself, *Can't he recognize the prophetic flow of the Holy Spirit? Look at the fruit—there are boxes and boxes of Kleenex being passed around.* The Spirit of the Lord was instructing, healing, and building up the Body of Christ. I felt agitation building in me. My next thought was, *Go away! Far, far away!* Then I screamed inside, *Stay away!* Exasperated, I thought, *Why are you here?*

But then I heard a strong voice whisper loudly to me, "We have a group of our youth who are about to go on a missions trip, and we need you to pray with them right now." With these words, he swung me around by the arm to face another group waiting with earnest expectation for the words of the Lord.

Still highly distracted, I began to pray. Right in front of me, wearing a stocking cap, sweatshirt and jeans, was an angelic-faced young person of 14 or 15. I was unsure whether the teen was male or female, but I started to pray, "Lord, bless *her* with wisdom...."

Immediately, the Holy Spirit said, "You are not even sure of this youth's gender!" However, they were about to load a bus and leave, and I felt the time pressure. I prayed quickly for several more of the youth, then spun around to face the waiting line of patient people. The Holy Spirit picked up where He had left off, and I rejoined Him in His flow.

LOVE COVERS

Later, to my horror, a trusted friend whispered in my ear, "The first young person you prayed for was not a girl, but a boy." My heart sank. All I could think of was the devastation affecting this young life. Part of me wanted to pretend that it had never happened, so I could look "super spiritual," but the greater part of me wanted to find the young man and ask his forgiveness. I wanted to explain that I had made a mistake by allowing myself to become distracted. I now know that, had I stood still, ignored the distraction, and waited upon the anointing of the Spirit of God, the mistake would not have occurred.

I had a choice to make: hold onto my pride or accept responsibility, correct the error, and make sure all was well with his soul. Turning to my trusted friend, I asked her to find the young man. I wanted to reassure him that the fault was mine, not God's or his. I wanted to explain that I was simply a human vessel distracted in the midst of the flow of God's Holy Spirit. Once again, I realized that my flesh profits nothing. More importantly, I must be led by the Spirit of God.

"Above all things have fervent love one for another, for 'love will cover a multitude of sins.' Be hospitable to one another without grumbling. As each one has received a gift, minister it one to another, as good stewards of the manifold grace of God" (1 Peter 4:8-10 NKJV). I almost robbed myself of an opportunity to learn an absolutely priceless, invaluable lesson. It's very simple: stay in the Spirit and always love God's people. Do not allow yourself to be distracted by the soulishness or the demands of man. Always, always remember that the person in front of you, in the time of prophetic ministry, is far more important than you; God is merely speaking through you to him or her. Keep your priorities in order. Guard people. Guard their souls, their spirits, and their minds through love and humility. Jesus set the example, on the night of His betrayal, by focusing on each one of His disciples through the act of washing their feet:

> *So after He had washed their feet, and had taken His garments, and was set down again, He said unto them, Know ye what I have done to you? Ye call me Master and Lord: and ye say well; for so I am. If I then, your Lord and Master, have washed your feet; ye also ought to wash one another's feet. For I have given you an example, that ye should do as I have done to you. Verily, verily, I say unto you, The servant is not greater than his lord; neither he that is sent greater than he that sent him. If ye know these things, happy are ye if ye do them* (John 13:12-17).

Remember, in a ministry setting, the Lord is focusing on the individual, not you.

Heavenly Father,

Thank You for the anointing You have given me. I ask You to open my eyes, ears, and spirit with Your enlightenment and under- standing. Help me to be supernaturally sensitive to Your Holy Spirit, just like Jesus. Help me stay in tune with the flow of the Holy Spirit. Jesus, I know You open the ears of the deaf, so would You please give me the ability to hear the voice of the Holy Spirit above all distractions around me. Help me stay focused and on guard. Let me love and embrace Your precious people and cover them with Your love.

In your Holy name, Amen.

MEDITATION SCRIPTURE

And I will pray the Father, and He shall give you another Comforter, that He may abide with you for ever; even the Spirit of truth; whom the world cannot receive, because it seeth Him not, nei- ther knoweth Him: but ye know Him; for He dwelleth with you, and shall be in you (John 14:16-17).

Devotional

Key Scriptures: 1 Corinthians 12:1; 2 Corinthians 4:7; John 7:38; Acts 2:15-18; 1 Peter 4:8-10; John 13:12-17.

Key Point: God will speak and place in our spirit (or "well") His thoughts, His words, His visions, His dreams. At the appointed time, He will release them under the anointing of the Holy Spirit.

DRAW FROM THE WELL

1. "The anointing is the _____ that draws the water out of your 'well.'"

2. If your spirit is the "well" and you feel a tugging on the rope, what does this mean?

   _____

   _____

3. *"He that believeth on Me, as the scripture hath said, out of his belly shall flow coffee/ rivers of living water/ tea/ milk/ new wine"* (John 7:38). (Circle one.)

4. What's a Holy Ghost "heads up"?

   _____

   _____

KNOW HIS DRAWING

5. "When you minister in the prophetic, you will feel the drawing of the Holy Spirit toward a certain person, just like "a _____ is drawn to _____.""

LOVE COVERS

6. *"Above all have _____ one for another, for '_____will cover a _____ of sins"* (1 Peter 4:8).

7. When you make a mistake prophetically because of distractions, what response should you have?

   a. Blame game
   b. Accept the responsibility
   c. Ignore it
   d. Defend yourself
   e. Deal with it
   f. b and e

CHAPTER 10

Prophetic Humility

THE INCIDENT

Staying in the flow of tattling on myself, I'd like to share more stories with you, hoping to prevent you from making similar mistakes. (If you have ever made a mistake, I'm sure I can count on your grace once again!) I'm glad to say many of my known mistakes happened years and years ago, for which I am very grateful!

I was in a group, the meeting was over, and we were closing in prayer. I felt impressed by the Holy Spirit to deliver a word to the group. It had been a wonderful night of worship, teaching, and praise. There was very strong agreement, releasing the flow of the love of God for one another. Boldly, yet cautiously, I began to speak out an unusually lengthy prophecy. At one point, I had to catch my breath.

Next, I heard pour from my mouth these words: "God is afraid." Mentally dissecting what I had just said, I began to argue with myself. I knew the Word of God, and that He is afraid of no one and nothing, because He is God.

In front of the group, I began to shake my head and say out loud, "No, God can't be afraid!"

Startled eyes popped open and puzzled looks came across faces. It seemed like a thousand years, but in reality was only moments. I had begun to listen and speak from my own understanding, rather than flowing and repeating what the Spirit of the Lord was saying. With a red face and a humiliated spirit, I became very quiet.

One of the other leaders, realizing I was faltering, said calmly, "Let's go back into the Spirit and listen to what He is speaking."

Still embarrassed but open to the Spirit, I continued on with the prophecy, "I am afraid for My people, for those who will be lost and will not come to the saving knowledge of My Son."

THE CAT'S MEOW

We then began to pray and intercede for the lost. The meeting came to an end shortly. What had happened was over, but it was far from forgotten. I questioned God and doubted myself. I remained embarrassed the more I thought about it. Slowly but surely, some of "Job's comforters" came over to offer *their* explanations. Still vulnerable and open, I was eager to receive their advice in order to prevent a repeat of such a humiliating incident—for Heaven's sake and for my dignity's sake as well.

Sister Such-and-Such, whose name shall remain anonymous, came strolling over smiling like a Cheshire cat ready to pounce on a mouse. I, the mouse, still had the cheese hanging out of my mouth! (Not one of my greatest moments.)

She purred, "The reason that happened to you was that you prophesy too much."

With a smile, or perhaps a sneer, I thanked her, but this humiliated mouse wanted to find a hole to hide in.

Quickly following in her paw marks, another one came prancing over. This woman began to gloat and offer unwanted advice.

"God just wanted to humble you to keep you from getting prideful."

I *really, really* just wanted to be left alone, so I could have my own "pity party" all to myself! This was a very bonding experience with my brother Job, for he also experienced such "purrfect friends."

Prophetic Humility

"WHAT HAPPENED?"

I wanted desperately to go home. Alone in my car, confused, and heavyhearted, I asked, "Lord, why did you allow *that* to happen, and *what* did happen?" I wanted to pull over to the curb in the dark and weep in humiliation. Hoping to receive some answers, I waited for His reply. I knew He would speak truth that would set me free. I wish I could say I waited with joy and anticipation, but that would be a lie. I waited in anger and embarrassment, because I was anticipating He would defend Himself. I was blaming Him for my humiliation.

But His great goodness overtook my self-pity and hurt.

He said, "You became like Peter. You stepped out of the boat and looked around. When nothing made sense, you began to falter and stopped. Then you became confused. There was no sin. It was very simple. You took a breath in the middle of a sentence, and began to reason in your mind."

Having been prophesying no more than six months, I was "learning the ropes." I was very immature in my gifting.

He continued, "Neither of those other women had truth, for they could not fully know your heart."

He showed me that His wisdom and grace had prevailed when we went back into the Spirit of agreement and received the fullness of the word. It was an extremely valuable lesson—humiliating, but worth the price. It taught me to relax in His presence and to flow in and enjoy His anointing. How Heaven must have laughed when I was ready to resign from the prophetic, because of breathing in the middle of a sentence! *"The steps of a good man are ordered by the Lord: and He delighteth in his way. Though he fall, he shall not be utterly cast down: for the Lord upholdeth him with His hand"* (Ps. 37:23-24).

These are small lessons that make a major point. The enemy will always gloat and magnify your mistakes, rather than show you any of your successes. It is important to realize the accuser of the brethren (satan) tries continuously to shut down the prophetic. The prophetic is

97

such an awesome gift, for it is the voice of the Lord God Almighty. We are privileged and honored to be His mouthpieces.

Heavenly Father,

I ask You to please break me of self-centeredness. Help me to grow in Your love and faith. I love being Your vessel, one through whom You have chosen to work and flow. Clean out my ungodly filtering system. Remove anything in me that would hinder the flow of Your will or Your voice from being declared upon the earth. I am so in love with You, and I realize You alone are Perfect Love. Help me to choose Your walk of love as You showed us when You walked on the earth. Thank You for hearing my prayer.

In Jesus' mighty name, Amen.

MEDITATION SCRIPTURE

Unto You I lift up my eyes, O You who dwell in the heavens. Behold, as the eyes of servants look to the hand of their masters, as the eyes of a maid to the hand of her mistress, so our eyes look to the Lord our God, until He has mercy on us (Psalm 123:1-2 NKJV).

Devotional

Key Scripture: Psalm 37:23-24.

Key Point: It is important to realize the accuser of the brethren tries continuously to shut down the prophetic. The prophetic is such an awesome gift, for it is the voice of the Lord God Almighty.

THE INCIDENT

1. If you falter while delivering a prophecy, what is one loving thing you can do? If this has ever happened to you, what did you do? Was it effective?

   _____

   _____

   _____

2. "Sister Such-and-Such, whose name shall remain anonymous, came strolling over smiling like a _____ ready to pounce on a mouse. I, the mouse, still had the _____ hanging out of my mouth."

"WHAT HAPPENED?"

3. The enemy will always gloat and magnify your mistakes, rather than show you any of your successes. It is important to realize the accuser of the brethren (satan) tries continuously to:

   a. Bait you
   b. Shut down the prophetic
   c. Intimidate you

CHAPTER 11

Becoming His Mouthpiece

STRONG REQUIREMENTS

It is a great gift to have agreement around you in order to flow with the Holy Spirit in prophecy. It would be ideal and awesome, but it is not always the case. Sometimes, you find yourself in a situation where there is a spirit of religion, which has dominance. Other times, there needs to be repentance for contempt of the prophetic. The fear of man can hinder the flow of the Holy Spirit.

Our first responsibility is to stay in His presence face to face in order to clearly hear His voice. This truly is the first requirement for being a mouthpiece for God. In God's presence, He imparts to His mouthpieces what He wants to impart to others, and then He provides the opportunities for them to do this. I would encourage all who are called to be a mouthpiece of the Lord to begin to pray for specifics and details. This will truly touch the hearts and change the lives of people, for our God is a very detailed God.

When Jesus met the woman at the well, He gave such specific details to her that she became an instant evangelist. Immediately, she went back to her town and told her neighbors she had met a man who knew everything about her. In fact, she said to Jesus, "*Sir, I perceive that You are a prophet*" (John 4:19 NKJV). She had come to draw water, but He had come to draw her unto Himself. He was fishing for her, and his bait was the prophetic. Not only did she nibble on the bait, but she swallowed

His words and received His life. Why? He served her an appetizing prophecy full of details and intimate revelation knowledge. He loved her enough to come her way and draw her apart from her life of sin. Again, what did He impart? Intimate details. *"Jesus said to her, 'Go, call your husband, and come here.' The woman answered and said, 'I have no husband.' Jesus said to her, 'You have well said, "I have no husband," for you have had five husbands, and the one you now have is not your husband; in that you spoke truly'"* (John 4:16-18 NKJV).

GONE FISHING

I use the term "fishing prophecy," hoping and praying none of us are guilty of "fishing too deep in the pond" beyond our measure of faith. This bait we must never use—the hearts and souls of God's precious people. To illustrate this "fishing" technique: the person ministering in the prophetic may scan the crowd, searching out information from different people in order to stir them up, so they can end with the declaration, "Thus saith the Lord." Later, the people may be wounded, scarred, and feeling abandoned by God. This is not His heart for His people. It happens when prophetic ministers begin to search out details beyond what Heaven has given. True prophecy should be inspired by God's Spirit and stay inspired from beginning to end.

I have seen prophetic persons grandstand and take on the attitude of high-mindedness or self-importance at the expense of others. They do this by using a common name, color, or general life experience—something that has not been given to them by the Spirit of the Lord. For example, such a person may say, "God has shown me that *everyone*—and I mean everyone—is going to be absolutely debt-free by such-and-such date"—a short-term, sensational deadline. The people give an emotional response like thunderous applause or victorious shouting.

Some of you may be thinking, *But with God all things are possible to those who believe.* Yes, God is God, so this is a true statement based on the Scripture. However, that's the upside view as long as God is truly speaking. This type of declaration has a downside, though. The immature in their discernment and faith walk may not grasp the portion of the word meant only for a certain group of people. Our God is a very personal God. The missing element is the personal responsibility of those who hear to discern what is of God and what is of man. It is extremely dangerous to bring a group or person to an emotionally charged state. This can bring people into the soulish realm and can encourage the prophetic person to operate from their ego rather than in the Spirit of the Lord. Why did Jesus hear from His Father in Heaven, "*This is My Son, in whom I am well pleased*"? He was fully led by the Spirit of the Lord.

Again, I caution the receiver *and* the giver of the prophetic to guard God's people. There are indeed times when an anointed, general declaration is spoken, a *rhema* word received by faith for certain individuals. We must always remain alert and open to receive from the Spirit of God when He is moving prophetically in a corporate setting. God loves when His people make a demand on what He has truly spoken. We do not want to ever be robbed of a gift or promise God offers to an individual or multiple individuals. This can create a celebratory environment explosive with the power and love of God, and brings glory and praise to His name.

We need to guard ourselves and others from falling into the trap of applying methods used by psychics to enthrall people and to further their personal kingdoms. They obviously are not receiving information from the Holy Spirit. Pure prophecy should not only point people to Jesus, His goodness and love, but should cause them to be drawn to Jesus in a deeper and more intimate way.

There are some prophetic people who, because of their higher level of faith and experience, do indeed receive accurate, wonderful insights; they use an appropriate, Spirit-led "fishing" method to confirm they are on the right track. Why? They are seeking to give the right word to the right person. These prophetic individuals step out of the boat to test the waters as they hear from God, even though they may not have a specific person attached to that word. For example, they may receive a prophecy, but not know at that specific moment which individual it applies to, until they speak it out loud and the receiver acknowledges it. A red flag should go up when the word is "murky" or inexact and does not connect to any person.

God's ways are higher and purer than our ways; so are His prophetic words. We should all establish this goal in our lives: to pray and ask God to purify the prophetic that flows through us to build up and empower His people with truth and healing.

AM I GOD'S MOUTHPIECE?

What is a good way to know if you are a prophetic mouthpiece? Look at your prophetic track record. Examine your heart to know whether God is calling you, or whether you have called yourself into this position. Is this really the position you are most highly anointed for in the Kingdom of God? You cannot judge this based on a few simple incidents. The Word says you prophesy according to your proportion of faith. "...*according to the grace that is given to us, let us use them: if prophecy, let us prophesy in proportion to our faith*" (Rom. 12:6 NKJV).

So, it would not be fair to judge your ability or gifting in comparison to others. They may have been prophesying from a higher level of faith. They may have progressively grown into and developed their gift through the years, after much practice and receiving confirmation reports. They have been hearing the voice of the Lord consistently and accurately. It is important to remember that at whatever level of faith you are prophesying, you should build on the same foundation based in His love. For even in Old Testament times, during the days of the great prophets, love was the motive that caused them to speak even harsh warnings.

It is wise to have around you strong, mature prophetic people who can encourage, pray, strengthen, and challenge you to attain a higher level of the prophetic. The higher level you obtain will bring a higher glory to the Kingdom of God on earth.

THE TWENTY YEAR FULFILLMENT

You display wisdom and humility when you allow others to hold you accountable for the prophetic words you have given; plus, it is a safeguard. I remember something a pastor's wife reported to me, when she phoned to invite me to their church. She had been inquiring of the Lord whether they should have me come. Near the altar after a service, she made casual conversation with church members.

One young man shared with her, "I hear you are thinking about inviting Eileen Fisher to come to our church. I would like to tell you that she spoke a prophecy over my life twenty years ago, and it is just now beginning to happen." He laughingly walked away, as though he had a secret. In fact, he did indeed have a secret. For 20 years, he had been hoping and desiring, although he was not quite sure that what had been spoken was true. Well, that had all changed, and he could laugh about it now.

As I write this, I smile, because I know that for 20 years he thought I had missed God. In all honesty, if this had happened to me, I would have thought the same!

The pastor's wife told me that within 15 minutes another lady approached her. She was very sweet, kind, and full of the love of God.

This lovely lady laughed as she said, "I understand you are thinking of inviting Eileen to our church. I must tell you she spoke a prophecy over my life with such great detail, and within ninety days it was totally fulfilled." (To God be the glory!)

The pastor's wife told me, "I knew without a doubt God was confirming to me that you were to minister at our church."

When she told me these things, I couldn't help but laugh out loud, thinking how good God is. He didn't let me carry the burden of making either of those prophecies come true. It is never the responsibility of the one giving the prophetic word to force the fulfillment of those words. A good job description of the prophetic is that we must deliver the right word to the right person at the right time.

Is the mail carrier responsible to pay a bill he or she delivers to you? Of course not! The addressee carries the responsibility for what is inside the envelope. Whoever seeks to force a prophecy to be fulfilled, can get trapped in a snare of trying to manipulate God, himself, and others through the gifting. More than once I have witnessed others say, "The Lord told me that you are to marry me"—then watched them stalk the person, trying to force and fulfill a soulish, ambitious prophecy. This obviously either came from their own soul or from the soul of another deceived person, rather than from God's Spirit.

When someone gives you a prophetic word, it should bear witness to your spirit that God has spoken. When Mary went to visit her cousin, Elisabeth's preborn son's spirit "quickened" and bore witness with the Holy Spirit. Within his mother's womb John the Baptist was joyously dancing in the Messiah's presence!

"*And it came to pass, that, when Elisabeth heard the salutation of Mary, the babe leaped in her womb; and Elisabeth was filled with the Holy Ghost*" (Luke 1:41). Confirmation brought comfort and encouragement to both Mary and Elisabeth. To John it brought unbridled joy. They all recognized and acknowledged the Holy Spirit had moved upon them. The lesson from these two women and "Prophet Babe John" regarding confirmations should keep you on the straight and narrow road, flowing in God's perfect prophetic will.

BLESSING OR ABUSE?

In the realm of finances, I have seen both the blessings as well as the abuse of prophecy. A friend once shared with me a distressing story. My friend was hosting a visitor from another nation. This man strolled into the room where my friend was sitting and confidently declared, "The Lord told me you are to give me a million dollars."

My friend chuckled and replied, "That's news to me. In fact, I don't even have it to give. If I did, I'd be up staring at it all night!"

The man retorted, "Well, maybe God said it was one hundred thousand dollars and five new cars."

My friend graciously and generously gave the man $2,500 and politely asked him to leave immediately. This is an extreme example of pure manipulation of the prophetic. Please forgive us, Lord!

I once received a phone call from a distraught lady. In a painful voice, she told me a horrifying story. She had watched a televangelist who promised all the viewers, "If you send in X amount of dollars (thousands), we will send you a personal prophecy...your very own word of the Lord."

Being in dire need, the woman sent this organization a check. Sure enough, a letter came back, but it was a general open letter that had probably been sent out to many, many others. Because she was so broken and desperate, she continued to send money—to the tune of $1,000 per month. She called me because she was running out of money. In fact, she was on the verge of losing her home and car. She had no idea what to do.

As I prayed for this precious lady, the Spirit spoke to me, "I am grieved by those who are prostituting the prophetic. I am about to release a severe judgment upon those robbing and financially raping the Bride of Christ."

My heart broke and grieved with Him. I knew that the experience of this woman and others was not the Holy Spirit, for He never comes to rob and destroy. Obviously, she did not use wisdom, but many times in desperate situations we are moved by fear above all else. Fear can be a calling card to greed and manipulation.

I relate these things not to take away from the true prophetic in any way, but only to show that the counterfeit is alive and well.

We are in the hour of the Lord's clarion call to the Body. His true mouthpieces must come forth to drown out the counterfeit sounds of the psychics, wolves in sheep's clothing, and all voices trying to rise above the voice of the Spirit of God.

FORGIVE US, LORD

It is time for us to repent to God's people, His priceless possessions, who have been injured and wounded by the prophetic. While a guest on Trinity Broadcasting Network's international "Praise the Lord" program hosted that night by Richard Hogue, I felt the Lord prompting me to look directly into the camera and say to the millions of viewers, "If any of you have ever been wounded or hurt at any time through the prophetic, please forgive us."

I could feel the pain, hurt, and grief coming back at me through the cameras. I knew in the spirit realm that the heart of the Spirit of God was to release all who had been held in captivity by wrongful prophetic words. Always remember...the wonderful voice of the Holy Spirit is the Spirit of Truth. These prophetic casualties would happen less often if we loved and cared more for God's treasured people.

A HOLE IN THE HEDGE

Prophetic people are not only called to give corporate and personal words like Jesus did to the woman at the well, but the prophets of old addressed kings, queens, and nations. We are called to prophetically intercede and "stand in the gap" for people and nations with the heart of God. "*So I sought for a man among them who would make a wall, and stand in the gap before Me on behalf of the land, that I should not destroy it; but I found no one*" (Ezek. 22:30 NKJV).

According to scholars, a "gap" was a break in the protective thorny hedge or wall of stones that surrounded a vineyard and invited trouble. To bar intruders, someone had to stand guard until the gap could be repaired. This is an awesome figure of speech to describe prophetic intercessors willing to stand between man and demonic assignments. A true intercessor blocks hostile fire from the enemy's camp and thwarts his ambitious, evil schemes.

Visualize with me a hole in the middle of a long hedgerow. Through this hole, an enemy illegally sneaks in and out of someone else's territory under the cloak of darkness. But he is discovered and apprehended by a watchman, who carries the legal authority to enforce his master's will. The watchman is willing to lay down his life to protect those placed under his care. He uses all his means and strength to fill the gap in the hedge, even to be beaten to the point of death, in order to guard the master's own. Why could he do this? He is under his master's jurisdiction, and his actions are authorized against illicit invaders. He's determined and willing to lay his life down, because he is deeply in love with his master and those loved by the master.

Our mission is to guard and build up the army of the Lord, just as the Lord Jesus, when He walked on the earth, built up His apostles and trained them in the ways of Heaven. I shudder to think of the fulfillment of these words of the Lord: "*Many will say to Me in that day, 'Lord, Lord, have we not prophesied in Your name, cast out demons in Your name, and done many wonders in Your name?' And then I will declare to them, 'I never knew you; depart from Me, you who practice lawlessness!'*" (Matt. 7:22-23 NKJV).

It is far better to lean toward loving and guarding people, than to run the risk of having to plead your case before the Lord: "Didn't I prophesy in Your name?"

It is so much richer for the sake of the Kingdom to say, "Lord, I loved, prophesied, and moved in signs and wonders, because I'm in love with You and Your people. All glory and honor goes to Your name. I know it is Your name that is above all other names."

Heavenly Father,

I ask You to touch my lips with a live coal, just as You did with Isaiah through your angel. Purify my mouth and put a guard over it. May my mouth never be a weapon that would destroy or offend You or Your Kingdom. Father, please let the fire of Your Spirit flow out of my mouth, thereby producing prophetic evangelism and intercession. I ask You now to please bring me opportunities to speak the life and the truth of Your Kingdom into the hearts of Your precious people. I ask You to help me and use me to confirm to others that they, too, have heard Your voice. I ask You to surround me with people filled with Your wisdom, knowledge, and faith. I pray You would send me someone to help mature me in the giftings I now lay at Your feet. Father, use me for Your glory and place me with the right person or people. May I have Your right word at the right time for Your namesake alone.

I ask these things in the precious name of Jesus, Amen.

MEDITATION SCRIPTURE

Then one of the seraphim flew to me, having in his hand a live coal which he had taken with the tongs from the altar. And he touched my mouth with it, and said; "Behold, this has touched your lips; your iniquity is taken away and your sin purged." Also, I heard the voice of the Lord, saying: "Whom shall I send, and who will go for Us?" Then I said, "Hear am I! Send me" (Isaiah 6:6-8).

Devotional

Key Scriptures: John 4:19; John 4:16-18; Romans 12:6; Luke 1:41; Ezekiel 22:30; Matthew 7:22-23.

Key Point: Pure prophecy should not only point people to Jesus, His goodness and love, but should cause them to be drawn to Jesus in a deeper and more intimate way.

STRONG REQUIREMENTS

1. It is a great gift to have agreement around you in order to flow with the Holy Spirit in prophecy. It would be ideal and awesome, but it is not always the case. True or False?

2. What is our first responsibility in the prophetic?

_____

_____

3. Was Jesus ever called a prophet? Give an example from the Scriptures.

_____

_____

_____

4. Circle the details in this Scripture that Jesus gave the woman at the well: "*Jesus said to her, 'Go, call your husband, and come here.' The woman answered and said, 'I have no husband.' Jesus said to her, 'You have well said, "I have no husband," for you have had five husbands, and the one whom you now have is not your husband; in that you spoke truly*" (John 4:16-18).

AM I GOD'S MOUTHPIECE?

5. "*...according to the _____ that is given to us, let us use them. If _____, let us _____ in proportion to our _____*" (Rom. 12:6).

6. During the Old Testament days, prophets who spoke even harsh warnings motivated by:

   a. Frustration
   b. Ambition
   c. Love
   d. Greed

THE TWENTY YEAR FULFILLMENT

7. "When someone gives you a prophetic word, it should bear witness to your spirit that God has spoken." True or False?

8. What happened to Elisabeth when Mary visited her?

   _____

   _____

   _____

BLESSING OR ABUSE?

9. "We are in the hour of the Lord's clarion call to the Body. His true mouthpieces must come forth to _____, _____ and _____."

FORGIVE US, LORD

10. What would cause fewer casualties in the prophetic?

_____

_____

_____

A HOLE IN THE HEDGE

11. "We are called to prophetically _____ and _____ for people and nations with the heart of God."

12. Are we all called to "stand in the gap"? Why?

_____

_____

_____

13. A true intercessor always:
    a. Blocks hostile fire
    b. Thwarts demonic ambitions and schemes
    c. Loves to worship
    d. Prays 24 hours a day and fasts daily
    e. a and b
    f. c and d

CHAPTER 12

Passing the Grade

SWEET LISA

The God-appointed position is always a safe place to be, especially when you are in submission to Him. If you have a need to be right, you leave the place of submission and enter the place of defense. When you become defensive, you put your guard up, and you are not being open and pliable. *Pliable* means "to be flexible and moldable." God sometimes places us in positions that stretch our faith to an uncomfortable level.

While attending a conference for ministers at Oral Roberts University in Tulsa, Oklahoma, I was invited to minister in the home of my new friend Lisa. She is a very precious, wonderful, sweet woman whom I had met earlier at the home of Solvey and Ken Henderson in Colorado Springs. I immediately fell in love with her sweet spirit and her love for the Word, His power, and the people of God.

I found waiting at Lisa's home a group of 20 to 30 people whom I had never met. As I surveyed the room, I immediately knew that God's presence was there. Why? The dessert table in the corner looked warm, delicious, and overflowing. (The dessert table alone bore witness to my spirit that I had heard God!)

Above the laughter and happy conversation of the people, Lisa announced it was time to sit down and begin the meeting. I looked around for a worship leader, because I knew there would be no way to flow in the spirit of prophecy without singing at least one song. This was the only way I had ever ministered...praise, worship, teaching, and prophecy—or at least worship and then prophecy. I was expecting someone, *anyone*, to break out in song to bring in the anointing so we could flow in prophecy. I thought surely they must be aware of this.

To my surprise, sweet little Lisa said, "Go ahead and start."

I thought, *Start what?* Having prophesied for well over ten years, I had never heard "Go ahead and start," except in the afterglow of music. Rather than look like I didn't know what I was doing; instead of saying, "Let's sing"; I hesitantly responded, "Yes, I'm ready. Are all of you?" (That was the most confident "hesitation" I had ever experienced in my life.)

In unison they replied, "Yes!"

I again looked around the room, this time really sizing up the situation. I thought, *Well, I might as well prophesy around the room from right to left. That way, I can't miss anybody.* Not quite sure this would even work, I glanced around for the closest exit. After all, we hadn't even sung the "Alleluia" or at least "Jesus Loves Me"! I sure could have used some reassurance right about then.

STILL NO ALLELUIA

I began to declare whatever God was showing me for each person. Yet, while speaking to the first person, the battle of self-doubt still raged inside me. I was secretly thinking, *Will this really work this way?* They all sat there open, receptive, and grateful. Then I heard sweet Lisa once again.

Before everyone and God, she asked the person to whom I had just given a word, "Was that true and was she hearing God? Did that mean anything to you?"

I was grateful to be sitting down—I was stunned! I was still missing the "Alleluia" chorus. The young woman who had just received the prophetic word smiled, with tears streaming down her cheeks. It was very evident the Holy Spirit had deeply ministered to her life.

Little did I suspect sweet Lisa would "play the devil's advocate" after each and every person. As the night dragged on, Lisa became the hammer in the hand of God, meticulously examining each and every prophetic word. I had a flashback to my experience with the "hot seat," only this time it felt even hotter. Unbeknownst to Lisa, God was mightily using her in my life that night to confirm to me the authenticity of the gift of prophecy the Holy Spirit had deposited in me. Now looking back over the years, I see that this was a most outstanding lesson, one that would forever impact and change my life. Today I say, "Thank you, sweet little Lisa." That night was a pruning night for me, but what a great location to have it happen.

I remember very clearly specific details being lavished on people that night. One young girl received words of encouragement to study law, that God was going use her in the judiciary system. It was apparent that she had come in with a heavy heart and was very discouraged. I had no idea what the heaviness was, so when Lisa asked her repetitive, inquiring questions about the prophecy, the young girl replied, "Yes, very much so. I am studying law and will continue until I become the lawyer God wants me to become."

The details grew in intensity as the night progressed. About halfway through the meeting, we took a much needed dessert break. Before enjoying my sweets, I visited my safe refuge, the bathroom. On my way to rejoin the group, I was just in time to overhear a conversation between two people I had prophesied over. They were unaware of my presence nearby.

One was saying to the other, "Can this be God? Does God really give those kinds of details, and can God really know that much about us?" Knowing some of the others and the details of the prophetic words, they were comparing notes.

I heard one girl say, "I'm not so sure it is God because of the personal details, so she might be a psychic."

I immediately ran back to the bathroom and whispered to the Lord, "I'm not a psychic, am I?" Confusion entered my heart and doubt rose up inside of me. After all, we still hadn't sung the "Alleluia."

I realized that the people receiving prophecy were being stretched. I silently screamed as I was being stretched as well. God reminded me of this Scripture: *"But the very hairs of your head are all numbered. Do not fear therefore; you are of more value than many sparrows"* (Luke 12:7 NKJV). I felt reassured that He knows the most intimate details of the hopes, dreams, joys, and sorrows of our lives.

FROM THE FRYING PAN INTO THE FIRE

My prophetic gift was placed in the fire and tested that night, but when it came out of the fire it carried the seal and approval of the Holy Spirit. Surprisingly to me, something else came with it—the fear of the Lord, which is the beginning of wisdom, according to Proverbs 1:7.

Up to this point, I had been very casual and comfortable moving in a traditional way with praise and worship, then teaching and prophecy— always in that order. I had thought the prophetic could only flow in this kind of environment. What happened in Lisa's home encouraged and humbled me beyond any other experience in my walk, because I knew there was no earthly way I could have known those things. I was total-ly dependant upon hearing the voice of the Lord and receiving all from Him.

As I reflected on it all later that night, my heart leaped for joy. I am sure that God orchestrated that night more for me than for them. They were blessed—which is wonderful—but I was twice blessed. He con-firmed my precious relationship with Him, and showed me that He wants to have the same intimate relationship with others. His promise to you is: *"You will show me the path of life; in Your presence is fullness of joy; at Your right hand are pleasures forevermore"* (Ps. 16:11 NKJV).

Heavenly Father,

I present myself to You and ask that You make me pliable. Mold me and position me for Your Kingdom's sake and glory. Break off all restrictions I have placed on You and the Holy Spirit through my own limited understanding. Please renew my mind and teach me Your ways. Help me to grow in understanding the vastness of You and Your power. I thank You for the times You've been patient and gentle in answering me, when I have presented foolish situations and questions from a self-righteous heart and a haughty spirit. Purify my heart, oh God...my spirit and my will...restore to me the joy of my salvation. Jesus, thank You for my salvation, for truly You are the Lover of my soul.

In Your Holy and precious, wonderful name, Amen.

MEDITATION SCRIPTURE

I will greatly rejoice in the Lord, my soul shall be joyful in my God; for He has clothed me with the garments of salvation, He has covered me with the robe of righteousness, as a bridegroom decks himself with ornaments, and as a bride adorns herself with her jewels. For as the earth brings forth its bud, as the garden causes the things that are sown in it to spring forth, so the Lord God will cause righteousness and praise to spring forth before all the nations (Isaiah 61:10-11 NKJV).

Devotional

Key Scriptures: Luke 12:7; Psalm 16:11.

Key Point: God sometimes places us in positions that stretch our faith to an uncomfortable level.

SWEET LISA

1. You always need to have praise and worship before prophesying in a group. True or False?

FROM THE FRYING PAN INTO THE FIRE

2. If your prophetic gift was placed in the fire and tested, hopefully it would come out with:

    _____

    _____

    _____

    _____

CHAPTER 13

A Time and Place

No Tape Recorders Allowed

It would be foolish for Isaiah to stand in the center of New York City today and prophesy the birth of Jesus, when it had already happened. So, be sure to have your words flow in the right season of the Holy Spirit. Inevitably, there may be times when you will offend some people who press in to receive a word. You must be free to say, "Yes, I do have the word of the Lord for you now"; or "No, the Lord is not giving me a word for you right now." I will give you an example.

One time while ministering at a conference, I was in dire need of a restroom break. I went straightaway to the ladies room, quickly found a stall and hurried about my business. In the stall next to me was a young woman, and I couldn't believe my ears when I heard her say, "Do you have the word of the Lord for me?"

Before I could answer, I saw a hand with a tape recorder coming at me from under the adjoining stall wall. It was the most startling encounter. In fact, it was the last thing I expected to have happen while occupying a restroom stall!

I quietly replied, "I don't think so. Not right now." After a few more hurried statements, I quickly finished and went out to join the conference. I'm not limiting God by saying where or when He will move on you to minister, because I do remember another bathroom event. However, it was a totally different scene.

NOT JUST ANOTHER MEAL

After another service, two pastors, one of their wives, and my husband and I had an appointment in another city with a pastor friend of mine. To my surprise, my pastor friend brought another couple with him to join us for lunch at a very busy and popular restaurant. I had no expectations of being super spiritual, for I assumed I was off-duty and was just going to have fun and laugh with friends. After all, it was Monday.

As we were eating our lunch in the middle of this busy restaurant, the Lord said, "I want you to give Mr. X (the pastor's friend) a word."

Between bites of my salad and baked potato, I declared over this man what God wanted to do through him and his ministry. At first, he looked taken aback; then he burst out crying loudly. Apparently, he was at a very low point in his life and his ministry. Now this was not just a "one liner" prophecy. I could sense the others at the table becoming very uncomfortable, as was I. It appeared that Mr. X could not quit crying.

I tried to lighten up the situation with humor, but it was very obvious to everyone he was going through deep "open heart surgery" by the Spirit of the Lord. Soon, God's surgery was complete and he began to laugh. Things seemed to return to normal. I started to relax and without missing a beat, continued eating, thinking this unusual event was over...so I thought. The Lord had other plans.

THE POWDER ROOM GATHERING

As I finished my meal, I heard the Lord say, "Invite his wife to the ladies' room."

So I invited my friend, Cindy, and the pastor's wife to join me in the ladies' room under the pretense of powdering our noses.

As the door closed behind us, the Lord said, "I brought her in here and I want you to speak to her heart so I can heal her, because she has so much pain and fear."

In this busy restaurant's ladies' room, Cindy and I stood on either side of this precious woman. As we prayed, we felt the power of God enter the room and begin to do heart surgery. She started to weep, as God removed layer after layer of pressures that had been put upon her. Yet, I felt the Lord wanted to go deeper. We continued to pray with our eyes closed, focusing on hearing the voice of the Lord. I waited, as He gave further instructions.

About this time, I heard the door open, but didn't even open my eyes to see who had come in. I didn't want to be distracted from hearing the voice of the Lord or from what He was doing. Suddenly out of nowhere, I heard a new voice—neither mine, nor Cindy's, nor the woman for whom we were praying. Just then, I felt someone grab my free hand and hold it with a firm grip. I still didn't open my eyes. (Thank God, earlier in my ministry I learned the hard lesson of how not to get distracted.) This anonymous lady was praying.

I asked the Lord "What is going on?"

I heard Him reply, "You needed reinforcements and stronger agreement, so I sent her in."

It was an amazing experience! God not only was in control of healing this woman's heart, but He was also in control of coordinating the perfect amount of prayer support to accomplish what He wanted done. As I said, "Amen" and finally opened my eyes, I looked into the face of this "new voice" shining with a brilliant smile, and the light and love of Jesus shining through her eyes.

God's Spirit is not limited to where and when He will minister. In our natural minds, we have established parameters of where, how, and when God will move. Here we stood, four women drawn by Him into the ladies' room where He, the Spirit of God, had joined us to heal and set this lady free.

We all learned a lesson that day. Brokenhearted people are close to the heart of the Father. He always, no matter where or when, longs to heal the brokenhearted and set the captives free. *"The Spirit of the Lord is upon Me, because He has anointed Me to preach the gospel to the poor; He has sent Me to heal the brokenhearted, to proclaim liberty to the captives and recovery of sight to the blind, to set at liberty those who are oppressed"* (Luke 4:18 NKJV).

Heavenly Father,

I thank You that You have created each and every one of us unique. Thank You for choosing me to join You in heavenly places and to laugh at the plans of the enemy. I ask You, Father, to go into those secret, hidden places where sorrow, pain, and fear are hiding, and flood them out of my life by Your visitation of anointed laughter. Father, I thank You that You long to laugh with me. So, I ask that You would give me a heart to respond to Your invitation as we laugh together in heavenly places. Truly, You are a victorious, eternal laughing Father, Brother, and Friend. I thank You , Lord, that when I'm in pain, you scoop me up and carry me. I praise You that Your joy has brought me strength.

In my Beloved's name, Amen.

MEDITATION SCRIPTURE

Then was our mouth filled with laughter, and our tongue with singing: then said they among the heathen, The Lord hath done great things for them (Psalm 126:2).

Devotional

Key Scripture: Luke 4:18.

Key Point: Be sure to have your words flow in the right season of the Holy Spirit.

No Tape Recorders Allowed

1. What are some of the personal boundaries you could establish to guard your personal life when ministering the prophetic? For example: keep my private time private, stay well rested, etc.

   _____

   _____

   _____

Powder Room Gathering

2. "God's Spirit is not _____ to _____ and _____ He will move."

CHAPTER 14

Warring With the Prophetic

I ONLY WISH

> *This charge I commit to you, son Timothy, according to the* **prophecies** *previously made concerning you, that by them you may* **wage the good warfare** (1 Timothy 1:18 NKJV).

Many people, after receiving a word of the Lord, expect it to happen automatically—like hitting a light switch and saying, "Let there be light." I only wish it were that simple. After a prophecy is spoken forth, it is tested. I have heard encouraging prophetic words spoken over people—that things were going to change for the better—only to hear later that things had gotten worse. When this type of scenario occurs, you have a choice: burn or toss out the prophecy, or pick it up and use it as a weapon of war. You may find yourself in the middle of a battle to stop the word from being fulfilled. One of the first definitions of the word *warfare* is "a military operation between enemies." War is an activity undertaken by one country or kingdom to weaken or destroy another.

We find ourselves warring here on earth to establish God's Kingdom on the earth. His Kingdom is established through the written Word and through the *rhema* word. Often, we do not understand why we are in this war, because we did not volunteer.

EMBRACING THE PROPHETIC

THE SWORD

Rhema implies that the Holy Spirit Himself has placed enlightenment on one particular Scripture, which leaps off the page and becomes alive. I call it the Holy Spirit's "flashlight." When this happens, the Holy Spirit is giving you the *logos* (written) and *rhema* (quickened) Word of God as a sword to be used in battle. We read in God's Word:

> *Therefore take up the whole armor of God, that you may be able to withstand in the evil day, and having done all, to stand. Stand therefore, having girded your waist with truth, having put on the breastplate of righteousness, and having shod your feet with the preparation of the gospel of peace; above all, taking the shield of faith with which you will be able to quench all the fiery darts of the wicked one. And take the helmet of salvation, and the sword of the Spirit, which is the word of God* (Ephesians 6:13-17 NKJV).

The Word of God, called the sword of the Spirit in this passage, refers to the *logos*, the *rhema*, or the prophetic word, upon which we either rest or stand. When we find ourselves with "battle fatigue syndrome," we should place the promises under the "pillow of our heart," then rest and delight ourselves in the goodness of God. This does not mean we have shut down our belief system; we are still exercising it on a more effective level during this delicate time. We are still in the battle of faith, but the tactics of war have changed. It is important we rest when we need to rest, and stand and fight when we need to stand and fight.

We may find ourselves exhausted from the battle, driven by fear and compelled to employ fleshly strategies. We may force ourselves into all night prayer sessions even when we feel sick or lack rest. We mistakenly think God will not move unless we stay awake and bombard Heaven. "Sleep fasts" only lead to more exhaustion and elusive victory. There may be short periods of night season prayers led by the Spirit for Heaven's purposes. But God knows our frailties.

One time during a worrisome season, I stayed up at night voicing fearful, panic-filled prayers. On one of those nights, the Lord told me to get some rest. Still in fear, I tried to take authority over satan and my flesh, determined to press on to daylight. However, God gave me a Scripture that night: *"He will not suffer thy foot to be moved: He that keepeth thee will not slumber. Behold, He that keepeth Israel shall neither slumber nor sleep"* (Ps. 121:3-4). After receiving this word, I decided that there was no need for both of us to stay awake, since I was extremely tired and He wasn't! I could still receive major breakthroughs, because my faith was in ready alert even while I slept.

TAKE IT OFF THE SHELF

I have heard a teaching that makes me shudder: "If you do not understand a prophecy, put it on a shelf and forget it." I think this is erroneous, and I don't believe it is what Paul taught Timothy. Would you shelve your Bible just because you didn't have total revelation or full understanding? It's outrageous to think you can win a war without using *all* your weapons. Even the devil knows the Word of God, so why would you consider letting him use God's sword on you?

> *Then the devil took Him up into the Holy City, set Him on the pinnacle of the temple, and said to Him, "If You are the Son of God, throw Yourself down. For **it is written**, 'He shall give His angels charge over You,' and, 'In their hands they shall bear You up, lest You dash Your foot against a stone.'" Jesus said to him, "**It is written again**, 'You shall not tempt the Lord your God'"* (Matthew 4:5-7 NKJV).

Jesus, in the middle of the temptation (warfare), never lost control. He stayed in charge by taking the upper hand. Jesus placed satan where he legally belonged, under His feet. He used the written Word as an offensive weapon to stop the enemy in his tracks. He made sure satan knew, in no uncertain terms, that He was God. In fact, Jesus declared to the enemy, "*You shall not tempt the Lord your God.*" He was reminding satan of his fallen state, and that He was still the only one true God.

The written Word of God is a double-edged sword, which can be used to build or destroy. The person's heart motive in speaking the Word of God is paramount and at times needs to be examined.

PULL UP YOUR BOOTSTRAPS

Paul counseled Timothy to "take charge." This means to put things in proper order. As a spiritual father to a son, Paul told Timothy to take full responsibility for the battle he found himself in and to go back, recall, and secure the equipment he needed for the battle. Paul was not taking on Timothy's battle. Like any good father, he knew part of his job was to exhort Timothy to mature in his gifts and the calling God had placed in *him*—not to pick up his neighbors', friends', or nation's prophesies, but everything personally given to Timothy himself.

He wanted Timothy to recall what had been spoken, but not yet fulfilled, as a way to propel him forward. "*Neglect not the gift that is in thee, which was given thee by prophecy, with the laying on of the hands of the presbytery. Meditate upon these things; give thyself wholly to them; that thy profiting may appear to all*" (1 Tim. 4:14-15).

Paul was not only encouraging Timothy, but was telling him to place a demand upon the prophetic words. He was also reminding Timothy that the laying on of hands by the eldership or presbytery had already released the agreement needed. Timothy was encouraged to fulfill his call in spite of his youth. Paul was insisting he not neglect the gift that was imparted to him. In other words, he was telling Timothy "Pull up your bootstraps and stir up the anointing already released in you for such a time as this." It was time for Timothy to learn, grow, and develop in the gifts of the Spirit.

Paul is still speaking the same message to the Church today. We are to stir up the anointing of what God has placed on the inside for others to confirm on the outside. How do we stir up the anointing within us? By pulling up our own "spiritual bootstraps" and vigorously running the race of faith. God has anointed, appointed, and equipped us with every-thing we need to fulfill our call.

God will place us in intense situations in order to force us to draw on Him, and to train our hands for war. *"Blessed be the Lord my Rock, who trains my hands for war, and my fingers for battle"* (Ps. 144:1 NKJV). Many of us think the anointing and moving in the gifts are with-out warfare. We need not focus on the enemy, or go around giving our agreement to others who brag about their battles with the enemy. We are called to brag about the reports and victories won through the Lord and Savior, Jesus Christ. *"I have fought the good fight, I have finished the race..."* (2 Tim. 4:7 NKJV).

ALL LEAVES CANCELED

We need to remain in the good fight of faith. We are not in a losing battle. We are victors in an already won war. Some situations try to hold us down in absolute defeat. We may be tempted to sit down under a juniper tree as Elijah did, thinking we can escape the battle for awhile. It is naïve and extremely presumptuous to think the battle between Heaven and hell might stop simply by wishing it away. It is a real world, with a real battle and a real devil—but more than that, with a real God. *"My lovingkindness and my fortress, my high tower and my deliverer, my shield and the One in whom I take refuge..."* (Ps. 144:2 NKJV).

We are not to take refuge in foreign, unconquered territory such as an unrenewed mind, self-pity, doubt, the fear of man, or even the strength of other people. We must acknowledge the Lord Jesus is our Rock of Ages: *"Jesus Christ the same yesterday, and today, and forever"* (Heb. 13:8).

Even as we mature, Jesus will always be our solid Rock. God may use circumstances, Scripture, or prophetic words to edify, encourage, and strengthen us. In the end, it should always point us back to the Lord our Rock. It is very important to place people, places, and things in a sub-ordinate position to Him. We must rise up and declare that Jesus Christ is Lord, our Victorious Warrior.

Heavenly Father,

I thank You, Lord, that You not only call me Your Bride, but that You call me to be a soldier in Your army, fully clothed and equipped to win each and every battle that comes into my life. Guard me from battle fatigue and fill me with Your Word, power, and wisdom. Show me which weapon to use in every battle. I ask You now, Father, for strategy for every battle that I or my household faces. Father, help me stay focused on You and Your Word. I choose at this very moment to stand in faith and agreement. I will brag about Your goodness and Your victories. All glory goes to Your name. Help me to fight the good fight of faith, never taking refuge in anything or anyone other than You. Aloud and with great authority, I agree and speak forth with all the heavenly hosts and saints that Jesus Christ truly has overcome the evil one. Father, I thank You that every battle I overcome is by the blood of the Lamb and the word of my testimony. Please break off the "wishy washy" testimony of my fleshly words and draw me into Your agreement.

All glory and praise to Your name, Amen.

MEDITATION SCRIPTURE

And they overcame him by the blood of the Lamb, and by the word of their testimony; and they loved not their lives unto the death (Revelation 12:11).

Devotional

Key Scriptures: 1 Timothy 1:18; Ephesians 6:13-17; Psalm 121:3-4; Matthew 4:5-7; 1 Timothy 4:14-15; Psalm 144:1; 2 Timothy 4:7; Psalm 144:2; Hebrews 13:8.

Key Point: God will place us in intense situations in order to force us to draw on Him, and to train our hands for war.

I ONLY WISH

1. According to prophecies previously made, Paul told Timothy to do what?

_____

_____

2. After a prophecy is spoken forth, it is generally tested. True or False?

3. What is the definition of warfare, and how does it apply to the spiritual realm?

_____

_____

_____

THE SWORD

4. Match and fill in the words that describe:

   Logos _____

   Rhema _____
      Written word
      Enlightenment
      Becomes alive
      Leaps out
      Black and white
      Greek
      Illuminated

TAKE IT OFF THE SHELF

5. Would you shelve your Bible just because you didn't have full understanding? Yes or No. Explain your answer.

   _____

   _____

   _____

6. Why did Jesus state, "It is written" and "It is written again"?

   _____

   _____

PULL UP YOUR BOOTSTRAPS

7. How do we stir up the anointing within us?

   _____

   _____

8. Which of these has God given us to fulfill our call?
   a. Anointing
   b. Equipping
   c. Appointing
   d. All of the above

ALL LEAVES CANCELED

9. "We are not in a _____. We are victors in an already _____."

CHAPTER 15

Winning the War

PLANET EARTH IS STILL PLANET EARTH

One day after a very busy schedule, I felt convicted because of my lack of time in prayer. When the Holy Spirit drew me into prayer, I repented for this lack. Deep in my heart, I had carried a secret unknown even to me...I was "puffed up," thinking God Almighty was in dire need of my prayers.

He replied teasingly, "The world can still go on even without your prayers." I knew He was smiling down on me, laughing while showing me the silliness of my self-important, "high horse" attitude.

We all know prayer is extremely important. The Word does *not* say, "Father, if You seek my kingdom first, I will be added unto You and everything I have." Yet subconsciously, many people carry this hidden thought. The real Scripture says, "*But seek first the kingdom of God and His righteousness, and all these things shall be added to you. Therefore do not worry about tomorrow, for tomorrow will worry about its own things. Sufficient for the day is its own trouble*" (Matt. 6:33-34 NKJV).

God tells us that even as we seek Him and His Kingdom, there will still be trouble. He also gives us a strategy for thinking about and handling a worrisome situation. I wish I could say I am untouched by worry. This is a goal I strive toward. Planet Earth is still planet Earth and it contains problems.

As soldiers in God's army, we must be equipped and ready. We must be standing on the Word of God and fighting worry, fear, and unbelief by taking our unredeemed thoughts into captivity. Start by firmly putting on your helmet of salvation, which will remind you of your identification with Christ. Like diligent soldiers preparing for war, you must wait to receive your marching orders. They will help to keep you in alignment with the direction of the Holy Spirit.

The Spirit leads the army of the Lord into each battle, then sustains us through the battle and on to victory. It is crucial to remember that we are all in the same army, even though each of us faces unique and different battles. It is important to know we can join together as His warriors, shoulder to shoulder, and agree with one another to bring forth victories. God's heart is that we celebrate together in each others' victories, learning from one another how best to fight.

> *Verily I say unto you, whatsoever you shall bind on earth shall be bound in heaven: and whatsoever you shall loose on earth shall be loosed in heaven. Again I say unto you, That if two of you shall agree on earth as touching anything that they shall ask, it shall be done for them of My Father which is in heaven. For where two or three are gathered together in My name, there am I in the midst of them* (Matthew 18:18-20).

GOOD WARFARE, BAD WARFARE

God watches over His words to perform them. Many of us today are fighting with poor warfare, not good warfare. This is how you know the difference. In poor warfare you gain nothing and continue to lose ground. In good warfare led by the Spirit of the Lord, you gain and maintain ground. Because of trials and tribulations in this life, we find ourselves continuously facing challenges. These challenges actually provide opportunities for us to become overcomers in Christ Jesus. The Word of God states, *"Yet in all these things we are more than conquerors through Him who loved us"* (Rom. 8:37 NKJV). *Strong's Concordance* defines *more than conquerors* as, "over and above; to conquer describes one who is super victorious and wins more than an ordinary victory, but who is overpowering in achieving abundant victory."

We need the most highly effective weapons to do the quickest and most effective warfare. In some situations, we may be battling a principality that is in operation. We need to pray and seek God for wisdom, knowledge, and revelation, asking Him to reveal any open door or doors that need to be slammed shut and locked.

It is crucial to keep faith and a good conscience, even when everybody else has rejected us and all that we may believe in. The apostle Paul encouraged Timothy in this regard: *"Having faith and a good conscience, which some having rejected, concerning the faith have suffered shipwreck"* (1 Tim. 1:19 NKJV). Paul's own testimony was, *"This being so, I myself always strive to have a conscience without offense toward God and men"* (Acts 24:16 NKJV). What is a good conscience? It is a pure heart without sin in our relationships with God and one another. Walking in lovingkindness will keep the doors locked against much of the warfare. We are commanded to love one another, for love is of God. *"And this commandment we have from Him: that he who loves God **must** love his brother also"* (1 John 4:21 NKJV).

A great spiritual exercise for each of us is to periodically examine our own conscience. Unforgiveness and unrepented sin cracks the door open, extending an invitation and giving access to the enemy. Jesus knew this, so He taught us how to pray, *"And lead us not into temptation, but deliver us from evil"* (Matt. 6:13a).

BETRAYAL IN THE RANKS

Satan is *not* all knowing; I am convinced that he obtains much of his information from brothers and sisters in the army of God. They have engaged in conversations on others' weaknesses and sins. We should never aid the enemy's camp by giving him secret information on fellow soldiers. There are names for such betrayals: gossip, slander, and backbiting. Remember that when you do this, the back you are biting is also the temple of the Holy Spirit; He dwells within that person.

"Having a good conscience, that when they defame you as evildoers, those who revile your good conduct in Christ may be ashamed" (1 Pet. 3:16 NKJV). It would be a great day, if Christians would join together in the army of God and form a solid, unbreakable band of loyalty and agreement with one another. We are told *"Finally, my brethren, be strong in the Lord, and in the power of His might"* (Eph. 6:10). There should be mutual strengthening as we look around and see other soldiers wearing the very same uniform we wear.

Imagine being sent off as a solitary soldier to a foreign land, then discovering a fellow comrade fighting for your country. More than likely, your common love of country would draw the two of you together in companionship. Let's take this one step further—imagine being captured by a strong enemy and cast into prison to be abandoned, abused, tortured, and forgotten. But then the prison door is fiercely thrown open and a brother in arms, screaming in pain, is flung into the dark, cold cell beside you. You would immediately do what you could to help him, and you both would find comfort in joining forces together.

In the spiritual realm, such camaraderie is called *agreement*, and it should be common in the Body of Christ. How the Spirit of God must be grieved when those clothed in the same uniform allow themselves to become objects in the hand of the enemy, to be used against brothers or sisters. Because the enemy is always looking for the weakest link, we must keep loyalty in the ranks.

Each of us should obey with utmost diligence the love walk. Jesus' banner over us is love, and love should be the slogan and battle cry for one another. Ponder this:

> *Finally, brethren, whatever things are true, whatever things are noble, whatever things are just, whatever things are pure, whatever things are lovely, whatever things are of good report, if there is any virtue and if there is anything praiseworthy—meditate on these things* (Philippians 4:8 NKJV).

WHAT IS A STRONGHOLD?

We must change our thought life and challenge others around us to do the same. In His Word, God shows us that we can find strength and agreement with one another, to abort the enemy's plans. The enemy wants to establish strongholds in our minds and footholds in our lives. Strongholds allow him to covertly operate under his title, "the accuser of the brethren."

Have you ever wondered how evil thoughts and temptations enter our minds and establish strongholds? First, a temptation itself is not a sin. But the goal of a temptation is to cause us to sin, thereby giving satan a foothold. Satan looks for ways to enter and set up dominion through our pride, the root of bitterness, unresolved anger, unforgiveness, disobedience, etc.

What is a stronghold? A stronghold can begin with a tiny seed of temptation, which takes root as a sprout, grows into a huge tree of sin, and wraps its restraining branches around us to choke out all life. Eventually, after we yield to sin over and over again, the enemy's foothold becomes stronger and stronger and establishes a stronghold.

Strong's Concordance defines *stronghold* as "a fortification or castle." The enemy lures us with the temptation, but with our habitual willful actions we freely choose to hand him the materials to build a hidden structure in our flesh and minds. He cannot build this stronghold unless we bring him the materials to do so.

An example of how a stronghold is built: Someone watches unclean movies—perhaps not vile or filthy, but unclean and tempting in nature. As he continues to yield to this habit, he chooses increasingly perverted movies. By now, he may not realize he is being drawn into pornography. Lust has taken root in his mind, heart, and spirit. By compromising purity and yielding to an unclean spirit, a very subtle and beguiling indulgence has led to a captivating, compulsive habit. A spirit of seduction keeps pulling and drawing on him until the stronghold of pornography, not his own choices, controls him. By his free will, he has adopted an impure lifestyle and given legal jurisdiction to a demon.

This does not need to happen. The Bible says:

For though we walk in the flesh, we do not war according to the flesh. For the weapons of our warfare are not carnal but mighty in God for pulling down strongholds, casting down arguments and every high thing that exalts itself against the knowledge of God, bringing every thought into captivity to the obedience of Christ (2 Corinthians 10:3-5 NKJV).

Heavenly Father,

I thank You for the power in Your Word, and that Jesus became the Word. I praise You that Your Word is alive and active. It is always moving on my behalf to accomplish Your purposes for me and my household. I thank You that not only Your Word, but Your knowledge and revelation shows me how to fight the good fight against the wiles and schemes of the enemy. Father, deliver me from all temptation that would try to trap me, rob me, and stop me from being able to run boldly to Your throne of grace. Let me understand the power of agreement that I carry and that others offer based on Your Word, in order to bring forth victory. Forgive me, Father, for pride, bitterness, anger, unforgiveness, and disobedience—or anything else that grieves Your heart. Just as You spoke of mustard seed faith causing the mountain to be cast into the sea, I ask You to please destroy any tiny seed of temptation in my life before it takes root and grows into sin. Help me to pull down any of my own arguments or high thing that would exalt itself against Your knowledge. Teach me to obey, that I may bring pleasure and joy to Your heart.

In Jesus' name, Amen.

MEDITATION SCRIPTURE

How can a young man cleanse his way? By taking heed according to Your word. With my whole heart I have sought You; Oh, let me not wander from Your commandments! Your Word I have hidden in my heart, that I might not sin against You. Blessed are You, O Lord! Teach me Your statutes. With my lips I have declared all the judgments of Your mouth. I have rejoiced in the way of Your testimonies, as much as in all riches. I will meditate on Your precepts, and contemplate Your ways. I will delight myself in Your statutes; I will not forget Your Word (Psalm 119:9-16).

Devotional

Key Scriptures: Matthew 6:33-34; Matthew 18:18-20; Romans 8:37; 1 Timothy 1:19; Acts 24:16; 1 John 4:21; Matthew 6:13; 1 Peter 3:16; Ephesians 6:10; Philippians 4:8; 2 Corinthians 10:3-5.

Key Point: It is important to know we can join together as His warriors, shoulder to shoulder, and agree with one another to bring forth victories.

PLANET EARTH IS STILL PLANET EARTH

1. As soldiers we should stand against:
    a. Worry
    b. Fear
    c. Unbelief
    d. Unredeemed thoughts
    e. All of the above

2. What's wrong with this statement: "God watches over His and my words to perform them"?

_____

_____

_____

GOOD WARFARE, BAD WARFARE

3. Describe what it means to be "more than a conqueror."

_____

_____

_____

4. Are Christians encouraged to fight? Yes or No. Find a Scripture to back up your answer.

_____

_____

5. *"This being so, I myself always strive to have a* _____ *toward God and men"* (Acts 24:16).

6. What is a spiritual exercise?

_____

_____

_____

BETRAYAL IN THE RANKS

7. How do we aid the enemy with information on each other in the army of God?

_____

_____

8. Satan is all knowing. True or False?

9. In the Body of Christ, what should be commonplace?

_____

_____

What Is a Stronghold?

10. "Satan looks for ways to enter and set up dominion through our
_____, the _____, _____,
_____, _____, etc."

11. How is a stronghold established in our lives?

_____

_____

_____

12. Who gives the enemy the materials to build a stronghold?

_____

_____

_____

CHAPTER 16

Survivors and Casualties of War

ONCE ABOUNCE A TIME

My father was a tall, full-blooded Irishman with black curly hair and bright piercing green eyes. To strangers he was known as Mr. Flanagan, but to us he was Daddy. When I was a little girl with curly hair and freckles, he loved to tell captivating stories which never began with "once upon a time," but "once *abounce* a time." I used to wonder why.

Sometimes, he would start a story without beginning with that silly phrase. Then, my two darling freckle-faced younger brothers, Willie and Tim, with one voice, would stop him and shout, "Daddy, you didn't say it, you didn't say it!"

They refused to let him proceed with the story until he started it all over again with "once abounce a time." I now realize this was our wise father's way of getting our attention. This funny phrase would spark our contagious laughter, and we eagerly awaited our dear father's special story. And so I begin this story...

Once abounce a time, there was a mother and a father who had a beautiful, courageous daughter. The daughter had a son named Garrett, a child with beautiful dark, wavy hair and gorgeous, huge brown eyes.

During the daughter's second pregnancy—a very exciting time but also a very scary time–she began to retain far too much body fluid for her heart to handle. It struggled greatly to pump this excess water. After successfully giving birth to a beautiful bald baby girl, Gabrielle, the mother went into cardiac arrest. Her heart had been so overworked, it doubled its normal size. She was immediately placed on life support systems. As a result, a very hopeless, strained-faced doctor came in and told her very anxious mother, father, family, and friends that he did not think this mother would live through the night. Unfortunately, this precious young woman also overheard two nurses confirm her death sentence: "Isn't this very sad? This beautiful young mother, who has just given birth to a baby girl, is now dying."

Because God loves and cares for this family very much, He began to release a series of miracles to cancel this declaration of death over the young mother.

"I SEE YOU!"

A dear family friend, Shirley, informed one of God's Generals, Pastor Dutch Sheets, of this tragic situation. Immediately, he answered the cry of a very distraught family and joined them in prayer.

Amazingly, when Shirley had entered the sanctuary of Pastor Sheets' church, she heard a prophecy: "God said, *'I see you!'*" She reported back to the family this powerful *rhema* word of comfort, which immediately brought a ray of hope to them. The young mother had just been placed in the ICU (*"I see you!"*). God wanted them to know beyond a shadow of a doubt that He was aware of their critical hour and was standing in their midst, ready to answer their cry for help.

God began mobilizing His prayer warriors, and suddenly 15 to 20 people, eager to fight the battle against death, arrived at the hospital. They began to speak Scriptures of healing. The Holy Spirit quickened promises and prophesies to be spoken over the young mother, who had not yet fulfilled all of her God-given destiny. The group continued to push back the advance of the enemy. They linked arms of faith and fought with boldness and determination. God saw their faithful hearts and began to fulfill His divine plan. Miracle after miracle exploded on the scene. He always watches over His word and prophecies to make sure they come to pass.

That night was the hottest battle of all fiery battles for this family. They used every weapon they could think of: the Word of God, the laying on of hands, the power of agreement, the gift of faith, prophecies not yet fulfilled, and the perseverance of the people of God. As the battle intensely raged throughout the night, prophesies were reclaimed as the Spirit of the Lord moved with authority and power. *"For the battle is the Lord's, and He will give you* [victory] *into our hands"* (1 Sam. 17:47b NKJV). He knew in advance that this battle would happen. He had established these prophecies in the past to be used this very night, as a powerful battleaxe, a mighty weapon. Within them was the promise of the future for this young mother. The Lord our Mighty Warrior had come to defend His own. He will also defend you.

Some stories' endings are sad, some are happy, and some leave you wondering. We have a "once abounce a time" happy ending. Mom, Dad, Momma and baby girl are all alive and well, almost nine years later. The bald baby now has beautiful long brunette hair, and the young mother's heart is stronger than ever before. How do I know all this? Because it is a true story about my daughter, Theresa, and our baby granddaughter, Gabby. It is a glorious testimony of God's miraculous power and faithfulness. God in His appointed "fullness of time" pulls forth His prophetic words, and uses them in our lives as a lifeline. Prophecy should produce life and keep life flowing forward.

TWO-SIDED COIN

Prophecy is like a two-sided coin. One side declares life; the flip side declares death. This next example is not a happy "once abounce a time" story. It is a sad but true account of false prophecy, and I wish it had never happened. False prophecy can have an appearance of credibility, but because it's of the devil, the fallout is pain, disappointment, destruction, and death.

This is the story of a 45-year-old woman married to a much younger man. A total hysterectomy had left her barren and unable to have children of her own. Before witnesses, a prophetic person had, with great authority, declared to this couple that the wife would bear a child—a miracle baby. Upon hearing these words, the young husband, with zeal and ambition, began to forcefully pressure her to take the intimate steps required to produce offspring.

Several years later, I met this lady for the first time. I had been ministering most of the day and again that night. It was about 11 p.m., and I was feeling exhausted and more than ready to go home. As I gathered my belongings, the Holy Spirit spoke to my heart and said, "Turn around and look at the lady who is at the altar crying."

The lights of the church were being turned off, so I had mixed feelings.

The Holy Spirit said, "Ask her why she is crying."

When I did, she began her story. "I am about to go through a divorce because my young husband is blaming and accusing me of rebellion and disobedience to God. He says this is why I can not get pregnant. I am at my wits end because of the prophetic word spoken over us. It has caused great division and constant fighting between us."

With tears streaming from her eyes, she asked me, "What do I do?"

I was not very quick to answer. I repeated her question to God, "Lord, what do I say?"

He replied, "This was not a word from Me. It was a fleshy word that was full of ambition and pride. It was spoken out, but not by My Spirit."

He told me to take authority, break off the words of the past, and release this woman from bondage and torment. Through the Spirit, I declared over her life-giving words full of hope. These words brought healing, liberty, and restoration of her dignity, her purpose, her identity, and her strength. He continued to show me how satan was operating through the soulish word of a man and had used it as a weapon against her and her husband to destroy their marriage.

HIS NAME IS AT STAKE

Satan is called the accuser of the brethren. It was very evident this was a false word, for it produced death…death to this woman's soul, her husband's soul, their marriage, and their agreement. It literally caused this woman to contemplate suicide.

We must always remember that our Great Shepherd, the Lord Jesus, has come to restore our souls. "*The Lord is my shepherd; I shall not want. He makes me to lie down in green pastures; He leads me beside the still waters. He restores my soul; He leads me in the paths of righteousness for His name's sake*" (Ps. 23:1-3 NKJV).

True prophecy must always be pure and undefiled for His name's sake. When you prophesy, you must realize you are doing it in His name. Remember, His name is at stake.

He does not come to destroy us, but to heal us. Perhaps one of the wrong elements in this prophetic word was immaturity in hearing correctly from God. Immature words can bring problems, heartache, and pain. People just starting out in the gift of prophecy must realize that there is safety and protection when they submit what they are hearing to someone more seasoned in the gifting. It is our responsibility to recognize the gravity of the situation that results from the operation of the prophetic gift. God is trusting people who move in the gift of prophecy with the hearts, minds, and souls of His most precious commodity—His very own people. The gift of prophecy should never bring confusion. It might not be fully understood at the moment, because we prophesy in part, but it should never bear the fruit of confusion. "*For God is not the author of confusion but of peace…*" (1 Cor. 14:33 NKJV).

Heavenly Father,

I ask You, in Your goodness and mercy, to make me aware and protective of the power held in the name of Jesus. Let me never bring confusion into people's lives, and let me never take them for granted. Help me always remember that Jesus, my Lord, is the Good Shepherd. Make me aware of any selfish ambition my flesh would have or any temptation that would arise from my heart that would exalt my name above Yours. Father, I ask for holy fear; that I would tremble in adoration and in awe of who You are and of Your power. When I don't understand why innocent and precious people get hurt or destroyed, may I still trust and know You are Almighty God. Father, for those of us who are weak and weary in battle, I ask You to release a new anointing and bring forth an extreme gift of perseverance, in order that Your name alone will be glorified. I worship You! You truly are the Alpha and Omega—my life is totally covered under Your omnipotence and omnipresence. I release into Your hands my past, present, and future. I trust You to bring about everything for my good—for the Kingdom and for all those seeking You with their whole hearts. Father, I thank You that You know all of my dreams, desires, and needs. I thank You that You answer me, even before I cry out to You. I cry out to You now and ask You to raise up many mighty voices in the prophetic, who will stand against all confusion, pain, and lies. I ask You to bring prophetic voices to heal, speak truth, and deposit peace. Above all else, may Your people fix their eyes on You and how deeply You love them. Thank You for loving us, guarding us, hearing our cries, and answering our prayers. I place my faith, hope, and future in Your care.

In Your faithful love and wonderful name, Amen.

MEDITATION SCRIPTURE

And we know that all things work together for good to them that love God, to them who are the called according to His purpose. For whom He did foreknow, He also did predestinate to be conformed to the image of His Son, that He might be the firstborn among many brethren. Moreover whom He did predestinate, them He also called: and whom He called, them He also justified: and whom He justified, them He also glorified. What shall we then say to these things? If God be for us, who can be against us? He that spared not His own Son, but delivered Him up for us all, how shall He not with Him also freely give us all things? Who shall lay any thing to the charge of God's elect? It is God that justifieth. Who is he that condemneth? It is Christ that died, yea rather, that is risen again, who is even at the right hand of God, who also maketh intercession for us. Who shall separate us from the love of Christ? shall tribulation, or distress, or persecution, or famine, or nakedness, or peril, or sword? As it is written, For Thy sake we are killed all the day long; we are accounted as sheep for the slaughter. Nay, in all these things we are more than conquerors through Him that loved us. For I am persuaded, that neither death, nor life, nor angels, nor principalities, nor powers, nor things present, nor things to come, nor height, nor depth, nor any other creature, shall be able to separate us from the love of God, which is in Christ Jesus our Lord (Romans 8:28-39).

Devotional

Key Scriptures: 1 Samuel 17:47b; Psalm 23:1-3; 1 Corinthians 14:33.

Key Point: God in His appointed "fullness of time" pulls forth His prophetic words, and uses them in our lives as a lifeline. Prophecy should produce life and keep life flowing forward.

"I SEE YOU"

1. What weapons were used to win victory in this battle?

    a. Word of God

    b. Laying on of hands

    c. Power of agreement

    d. Gift of faith

    e. Prophecies yet to be fulfilled

    f. Perseverance

    g. All of the above

TWO-SIDED COIN

2   "This was not a word from Me. It was a fleshly word that was full of _____ and _____. It was spoken out, but not by _____."

3. What kind of words does the Spirit of God declare over people's lives?

_____

_____

_____

His Name Is at Stake

4. "True prophecy must always be pure and undefiled for His name-sake." True or False?

5. "The gift of prophecy should never bring confusion." What Scripture confirms this statement?

_____

_____

_____

CHAPTER 17

Prophetic Visions and Dreams

THE "IF"

Several years ago during my prayer time, the Lord gave me a vision. Now some of you may ask, "What is a vision?" According to *Webster's Dictionary*, a *vision* is "something seen otherwise than by ordinary sight (as in a dream or a trance)." Some people may say visions are in "your mind's eye," but I would say many visions are perceived in "the mind's eye of your spirit." All of God's visions are seen and received through your spirit. Visions come in many forms, but the intention of this book is not to elaborate or expound on them.

The Scripture is full of visions, some good and some bad. The Lord explains, "*...If there is a prophet among you, I, the Lord, make Myself known to him in a vision; I speak to him in a dream*" (Num. 12:6 NKJV).

It's interesting to note the order in this Scripture. The word *if* stands out to me because it qualifies the presence of a prophet, just as prophecies are conditional. God can declare His highest will; yet man's will can still blatantly oppose, block, delay, or cancel what the Lord has proposed to do. I have been asked, "Is it possible for true prophecy not to be fulfilled?" My answer is that many of God's prophecies and promises are conditional. An example is, "*If My people who are called by My name w* *humble themselves, and pray and seek My face, and turn from their wicked ways, **then** I will hear from heaven, and will forgive their sin and heal their land"* (2 Chron. 7:14 NKJV).

"JESUS LOVES YOU"

We know that God's desire, stated in John 3:16, is for all to be saved, but not all will be saved. Why not? Because they may use their free will and oppose God's highest, most perfect will for humankind. God was willing to run the risk of losing some, in order to gain others who choose to accept and come under His Lordship. An awesome way to pray for those who refuse to receive the Lordship of Christ is to ask Him to make Himself known. God answers this request in multiple ways. Perhaps He will bring a vision or dream. He may send someone to witness to another person by saying, "Jesus loves you," and sharing their testimony. The hearer may or may not receive the words, depending on their heart.

God longs to make Himself known to those He has created, because they were created for His good pleasure. He paid the price of His life for them on the Cross. God still speaks in visions, dreams, and words through His prophets and His prophetic people, who repeat or replay what they have heard or seen for others to receive or reject. Our free will is the deciding factor in receiving prophesies as well as salvation. We must cooperate with God's way of doing things.

FLY THE ANOINTED SKIES

I had been saved only one year and was still carrying around my big black Bible, armed and ready to convert anyone or anything that moved. I was faithfully attending a weekly ladies' Bible study taught by a kind and loving Episcopalian nun. In those days, I looked like I had just stepped out of the "discount outlet of the month" fashion catalog. My makeup was layered on thick, and I did not give the appearance of a natural beauty. I was put together with colorfully dyed hair and long fake eyelashes, recently purchased at the five-and-ten store.

This particular week, I expectantly arrived, hurried down the stairs to the church basement and started scoping out a great seat close the teacher. I was there for one reason—to grow into a mighty woman of God and save the world from their sin. My main motivation was for me and me alone. Even though I wanted to convert everybody, I wanted nothing to do with evangelism here in *my* secret haven of knowledge.

The room quickly filled up as I talked and visited with my friends. I definitely was not seeking out new gals to befriend or socialize with, even though, I'll admit, I wished someone else had my "fashion sense." Most attendees at these meetings were average housewives—not beauty queens.

Suddenly, in the doorway appeared a drop dead gorgeous 5'10? woman who looked like an ex-playboy bunny. She sacheted in with her wavy, thick auburn hair (natural of course), perfect facial features—high cheekbones, pouty lips, huge eyes—the works. And there they were…long, luscious eyelashes. The major difference between her and me—her beauty was naturally real! Her lovely eyes fluttered across the room, obviously seeking someone like herself. Lo and behold, she smiled at me with her perfect white teeth and made her way through the crowd toward me!

"Excuse me, excuse me," she politely said as she skirted around the clusters of women. She and her full-length fur coat needed plenty of berth.

She gushed at me, "Hi, I'm Tiffany. I knew you were friendly the moment I saw you, and I wanted you as my friend. Want to have lunch after the meeting?"

I smiled weakly back at her, not so sure being friends was the best idea or that I wanted to accept her lunch invitation. My next thought was, *I have absolutely nothing in common with you.* After all, I had never owned a real fur coat.

As the Bible study started, Tiffany and her coat settled in comfortably next to me. I became very distracted by the oversized, brilliant dia monds flashing off her fingers and reflecting off her earlobes. My simp gold wedding band was such a stark contrast to her fancy rings. V uncomfortable, I was convinced we would never hit it off. I also made an emphatic decision not to have lunch with her, either.

Before I knew what was happening, she reached over and blatantly wrote "Tiffany" and her phone number in my notebook! This woman did not take a hint! Then she had the audacity to write my name in her own notebook with a question mark. I gave her a fake smile and reluctantly wrote down my phone number. A familiar cliché flashed across my mind: "Do not judge a book by its cover."

Later at home during dinnertime after a busy afternoon of appointments, the dreaded phone call came.

Tiffany's excited voice sang into the receiver, "Hi Eileen, this is Tiffany. I told you I would call! I always keep my promises." I turned my dinner on simmer and sincerely listened to this lonely, beautiful woman as she poured out her heart. To my surprise, the more she talked, the more I felt like a protective mother.

Tiffany told me, "I just moved here from Las Vegas. I used to be a playboy bunny, but then I met Jesus and got saved. I got fired from my job because when the girls ended their performances, I would stand at the stage door and hand out tracts to them. I'd smile at each one and say, 'Jesus loves you.' I know I needed to quit, so I was relieved when my boss fired me. But my real problem is this: while a playboy bunny, I met my unsaved husband at the club. He's a corporate multi-millionaire and now he always tells me, 'I married a playboy bunny, not a religious fanatic.' We've been living like this for a couple of years. Will you come and pray for him?"

After hearing all this, I said, "I'll pray and ask the Lord if it's me who should pray with him or someone else."

Intimidated by our huge financial differences, I thought it would make more sense for God to send another "jet setter" who could more easily relate to him. At least she and I could relate because of our lashes, hair, and passion for Jesus!

She continued, "He owns his own jet and will be flying home next ekend. Can you come then?"

Not wanting to discourage her, I replied, "I'll pray *for* him."

The next morning, the Holy Spirit firmly reminded me of my promise. I earnestly set about my assignment to pray for this precious girl's husband. I had no idea where to start. So, I prayed very simply, "Lord, help him and show him Your truth"—a universal, generic, safe prayer.

Even as I prayed this way, I felt the Holy Spirit nudge me to be still, because *He* wanted to pray through me. This went on for several days, and I became increasingly frustrated because I knew I was missing the mark. Still, a promise is a promise, so I continued. The day of the husband's arrival was looming over me, and I knew I needed some answers.

Then, I clearly heard the Holy Spirit say, "Fast and pray." The next morning, I started a three-day water fast. Certainly, this would make God speak to me. Three long days later, still no answer. I went off to bed, knowing that Tiffany was waiting for my call.

That third night, I fell asleep and had a dream. This dream was different...it was a God-given dream. How do I know this? Jesus came to speak with me in this dream. I wish I could say this happens nightly, but it doesn't. Anyway, in this dream Jesus and I were riding in a private jet. We were alone, laughing and talking in the main cabin.

Suddenly, Jesus said, "Go up front and look at the pilot."

I got up and walked to the front of the airplane. There was the pilot, laughing and joking as though he were on top of the world and loving every minute of it. He obviously had no interest in any dramatic life changes. He smiled at me, and I smiled back; however, I sensed an empty, stony heart deep within him.

When I returned to my seat, Jesus said, "He wants no changes, but he also does not know where he's heading (hell). I want you to tell Tiffany that he has no desire to change, and I am honoring his free will. You are to give her these Scriptures to use in prayer as a weapon to pull down strongholds and come against the darkness so he will be able to hear truth."

Immediately, I woke up with a start.

The next morning, I did as the Lord instructed and told Tiffany I would not be coming over to witness to him. I told her God had showed me in a dream that He heard the cries of her heart. Jesus was taking her into a season of prayer and giving her the weapons to combat the foolishness in her husband's life.

I wish I could tell you the ending to this story, but I can't: with the passing of time, I have lost contact with Tiffany. However, I do know God is the Author and Finisher of our faith. God authorized this dream and gave Tiffany the ammunition necessary to pray for her husband. I believe her prayers were answered. Some of you have loved ones in the same situation as Tiffany's husband. I encourage you to seek the Holy Spirit's counsel about how to pray for them. Ask Him to release the gift of faith in your life, because all of us are given a measure of faith.

PERMISSIVE WILL VERSUS PERFECT WILL

I remember as a little girl being taught about God's permissive will versus His perfect will. I wondered about the difference. I would say I have come to a partial understanding. I offer this concept of God's perfect and permissive wills, not as dogma, but as something to ponder and meditate upon.

An example of God's perfect will is Jesus. As a man, Jesus was perfect in every way, in His obedience and total surrender to the Father's will. He did only what the Father showed Him. This means that He always strived for and attained God's perfect or highest will. All prophesies were totally and absolutely fulfilled regarding His birth, ministry, death, and resurrection. He always stayed focused and in God's perfection. He did not have a wandering eye or a wondering heart. Satan came to thwart the fulfillment of these prophesies by tempting Jesus to sin. But satan failed because Jesus had no sin, no disobedience, and no rebellion in Him—only purity and submission to the Father. Jesus was never ever in God's permissive will—He was conceived, born, ordained, crucified, and resurrected in God's perfect will. No one other than the Son of God will ever be able to say this.

Mankind, on the other hand, was born with original sin and so easily slips into rebellion. However, the redeemed children of God are expected to diligently strive after God's perfect will. To the degree that we do so, we are candidates to potentially see fulfilled every prophecy spoken over our lives by God's Spirit. Many people give only nominal or mental assent to God's perfect will for their lives, and instead choose to dwell in God's permissive will. The latter can cause many prophecies to remain unfulfilled. This happens by the choices we make, such as marriage or career decisions, etc. In His permissive will, our choices are based on decisions we make in our flesh, rather than directed by God's Spirit.

Thus, our choices in the "natural" have a definitive impact on whether true prophetic words are fulfilled. For example, a married woman receives a prophecy that God wants her to bear a child. Rather than receiving this word in her spirit, she takes measures to never get pregnant. She is asserting her own will, which blocks God's will. Choice is a huge factor when it comes to seeing prophecies fulfilled. In the garden of Gethsemane, Jesus, as a man, had free will like the rest of us. He could have aborted the earthly mission He was sent to accomplish. But He made the right choice.

The Mind's Eye

God will get our attention when He desires to show us things in the Spirit realm that He wants manifested in the natural realm.

I remember, as a little girl in school, the anticipation and excitement that filled us when the teacher brought an old, huge, heavy black projector into the classroom. Knowing that we were about to be treated to a new, fun movie or a documentary, we giggled and clapped our hands with joy. After turning the reel around and around to rewind the film, and firmly popping it back onto the projector, the teacher would tell one of the children, "Pull the blinds down and turn off the lights." Then, "Sssshhh, children...or you won't hear the movie."

God uses the same principle in our "mind's eye," especially in the prophetic gifting.

He says, "Sssshhh, be still...listen carefully...see precisely...speak accurately...only what has been shown and spoken to you." It's just like watching a movie or a still shot from a movie. This is how God works with us through visions.

After His vision is cast upon our spirit, the Spirit of enlightenment dims the light in our mind's eye, so we can clearly see His projection—either on the screen of our mind or with our natural eyes. This is what happens throughout Scripture. Many times with "open visions," it is as though a neon sign or picture is hung out in midair for us to view. Does this sound crazy? Absolutely!

> *But the natural man receiveth not the things of the Spirit of God: for they are foolishness unto him: neither can he know them, because they are spiritually discerned. But he that is spiritual judgeth all things, yet he himself is judged of no one. For who hath known the mind of the Lord, that he may instruct Him? But we have the mind of Christ* (1 Corinthians 2:14-16).

DOES THIS SOUND CRAZY?

I can hear some of you laughing, some at me and some with me. Those of you who have had visions are saying, "Yes and amen." You who have never heard of or experienced visions may think, "Let's call the paddy wagon and get the straightjacket." When I first had a vision, I thought I was losing my mind. I share these things with you, not to prove or disprove I am crazy, but to help you understand. The spirit realm operates completely different from the natural realm. I encourage you to do a Bible search on the word *vision(s)*. You will discover them repeatedly throughout the Bible—beginning in Genesis 15:1 with Abraham, and continuing right through to John's vision of horses in Revelation 9:17.

JUST ASK PETER

When God gives a vision, He gives it for a purpose, and He wants to give us interpretation and understanding of that vision. There is a saying, "A picture is worth a thousand words." It is the same with visions— they impacted the spreading of the Gospel to the Gentiles. If you don't believe me, read what happened to Peter: "...*he* [Peter] *fell into a trance. ...Now while Peter doubted in himself what this **vision** which he had seen should mean...*" (Acts 10:10,17).

It is interesting to note that the prophet Daniel said he sought for the meaning. "*And it came to pass, when I, even I Daniel, had seen the **vision**, and sought for the meaning, then, behold, there stood before me as the appearance of a man*" (Dan. 8:15).

Receiving visions involves a twofold process. One is to receive, and the other is to pray or fast if needed to receive interpretation of the vision. Daniel said, "*there stood before me as the appearance of a man.*" He did not state that an actual man stood before him, but he knew this by the spirit of revelation and the subsequent interpretation. In our flesh we can create and bring about our own visions by our own imagination. This is not the same as when God deposits His heavenly visions into our spirit.

There may be a lapse in time between the receiving and the fulfillment of a vision. Similarly, there may be lapses in time between speaking forth a word and seeing the word come to fulfillment. "*Write the vision, and make it plain upon tables, that he may run that readeth it. For the vision is yet for an appointed time, but at the end it shall speak, and not lie: though it tarry, wait for it; because it will surely come, it will not tarry*" (Hab. 2:2-3).

So what are we instructed to do with visions? We are told to make them plain. Write it down and run with it (which means to ponder it in your heart). Then, we are instructed to read it. With many visions, just like with prophecies, God desires we mix our faith with agreement to bring them to fulfillment. Prophecies and visions give us a "point of contact" to see, hear, and proclaim the Kingdom of God on earth. Part of the job description of a prophet is to figuratively hold up signpost with instructions and directions, pointing people to God's Kingd purposes. The reason I have belabored this point on visions is to lay a foundation for the vision I am about to share.

THE VISION

While in prayer, the Lord showed me a huge, ancient Roman arena like the Coliseum, where Christians were thrown to the lions for the entertainment of the Roman audience. God told me to look into the grandstands. Where normally thousands of people would be cheering, the seats were more than half empty.

I said, "Lord, what are you showing me?"

He said, "Many of My prophets have left the arena."

I said, "Lord, *where are the prophets?*"

He answered, "They were beaten up, and now they are discouraged and weary. They are hiding out in caves. I want you to call back the prophets into the arena. I am sounding a trumpet that they alone will recognize. I long to bring them back together...to bring one voice of agreement...to establish My glory across the face of the earth."

He began to reveal to me that the prophet's mouths had become silent, and the Kingdom of God was not flowing at its highest level. He showed me His divine strategy for when prophets are in position and making declarations by the Spirit of the Lord. Intercessors then pray through to establish these prophetic decrees, so the manifestation comes quickly and the flow of His Spirit is unbroken.

Heavenly Father,

> *Please forgive me for all the times I have chosen to make myself unavailable to the Holy Spirit's beckoning. Today I ask You to begin to develop in me a tender heart and also to give me the gift of a "tough skin." May the words and opinions of people neither persuade nor cripple me. Do not allow me to be susceptible to those flattering me with corruption or condemning me with criticism. Open the eyes of my spirit, so I can see what You would have me see, whether the heart of the person in front of me or an open vision like You gave to*

Peter. Confirm visions and dreams to me, just like You did with Peter and the prophets.

Your Word says You have no favorites. I ask You for the gift of being sensitive to those things that are happening all around me in the spiritual realm. Guard me from all foolishness and arrogance. Please keep me humble and give me a pure and clean heart, so You can trust me with greater spiritual revelation and secrets from the precious Holy Spirit. Give me the ability not to take myself so seriously that I would be robbed of the joy of my salvation. I choose to join You as You share visions and dreams from Your heart with me. Father, move me into Your perfect will. Thank You for creating me for Your good pleasure. Giving You the gift of my free will, I ask You to use it to declare Your Kingdom upon the face of the earth. To You be the glory and praise for Your mighty and wondrous deeds.

In Your mighty name, Amen.

MEDITATION SCRIPTURE

But God hath revealed them unto us by His Spirit: for the Spirit searcheth all things, yea, the deep things of God. For what man knoweth the things of a man, save the spirit of man which is in him? even so the things of God knoweth no man, but the Spirit of God. Now we have received, not the spirit of the world, but the spirit which is of God; that we might know the things that are freely given to us of God. Which things also we speak, not in the words which man's wisdom teacheth, but which the Holy Ghost teacheth; comparing spiritual things with spiritual. But the natural man receiveth not the things of the Spirit of God: for they are foolishness unto him: neither can he know them, because they are spiritually discerned. But he that is spiritual judgeth all things, yet he himself is judged of no man. For who hath known the mind of the Lord, that he may instruct Him? But we have the mind of Christ (1 Corinthians 2:10-16).

Devotional

Key Scriptures: Numbers 12:6; 2 Chronicles 7:14; 1 Corinthians 2:14-16; Genesis 15:1; Revelation 9:17; Acts 10:10-17; Daniel 8:15; Habakkuk 2:2-3.

Key Point: He began to reveal to me that the prophet's mouths had become silent, and the Kingdom of God was not flowing at its highest level. He showed me His divine strategy for when prophets are in position and making declarations by the Spirit of the Lord.

THE "IF"

1. What is a vision?

_____

_____

_____

2. Is it possible for true prophecy not to be fulfilled? Yes or No.

"JESUS LOVES YOU"

"Man's _____ _____ is the deciding factor in receiving prophesies as well as salvation."

FLY THE ANOINTED SKIES

4. Does God authorize dreams so we can pray for loved ones? Yes or No.

PERMISSIVE WILL VERSUS PERFECT WILL

5. Give an example of God's perfect will.

_____

_____

_____

6. Was Jesus in God's perfect will or permissive will? (Circle one.)

7. "Our choices in the '_____' have a definitive impact on whether true prophetic words are fulfilled."

THE MIND'S EYE

8. Visions are like watching a movie. God uses similar steps in our "mind's eye" for the prophetic gifting. What are those steps?
   a. Be still
   b. Listen carefully
   c. See precisely
   d. Speak accurately
   e. All of the above

9. Describe an "open vision."

_____

_____

_____

10. "The natural man can receive the things of the Spirit of God." True or False?

DOES THIS SOUND CRAZY?

11. "The spirit realm operates completely different from the natural realm." True or False?

JUST ASK PETER

12. After Peter fell into a trance did he fall out the window or did he see a vision? (Circle one.)

13. What did Daniel and Peter have in common?
    a. Cast into prison
    b. Visions
    c. Supernaturally set free
    d. All of the above

14. What were the two things Daniel did after receiving a vision?

_____

_____

_____

15. Do we *run with a vision* or *sit on a vision* or *stand on a vision or write down a vision?* (Underline one or more.)

16. At appointed times do visions speak? Yes or No.

17. Sometimes we need to wait on a vision for it to come to pass. True or False?

THE VISION

18. What is God's divine strategy for when prophets are in position and making declarations by His Spirit?
    a. Intercessors pray to establish prophetic decrees
    b. Manifestations of prayer requests come quickly
    c. Flow of His Spirit is unbroken
    d. None of the above
    e. All of the above

19. For the Word says, "*All may prophesy.*" True or False?

20. Do those in the office of the prophet only prophesy over leaders, nations, presidents, rulers, and kings? Yes or No.

_____

_____

_____

CHAPTER 18

Where Are the Prophets?

CALLING ALL PROPHETS

There is a stark difference between moving in the gift of prophecy, given as the Holy Spirit wills, and standing in the office of a prophet, which is part of the fivefold ministry. For the Word says, *all may prophesy.* (See First Corinthians 14:31.) However, prophets are called to occupy the office and receive God's delegated authority given to His mouthpieces. Usually, the one who stands in the office of prophet prophesies over leaders, nations, presidents, and kings, as well as to individuals or churches. Prophets move in a higher unction and anointing than those who prophesy occasionally as the Holy Spirit wills.

In the previous chapter, I shared a vision regarding prophets who have left the "arena." I feel very sorrowful, because the Holy Spirit is longing for those who are called to prophesy to return and be at the forefront of Heaven's business. Many people who at one time were prophesying and called to occupy the office of a prophet, have become offended, wounded, and discouraged through weariness. There are many different reasons why this has happened, just as there are different types of people hiding in the "cave." Some have legitimate reasons for being there and some should never leave the cave. Some of you are coming out walking in purity in this office and gift, because you've final' faced the issues that drove you into the cave.

A new sound is coming from the Spirit of God, just as a new sound came on the day of Pentecost when the Holy Spirit came as a mighty rushing wind. The battle cry this time is different. In the spiritual realm, there is a stirring...the stirring of God's glory. It will be a weighty manifestation of His presence. Prophetic voices are those called to be the heralds of good news. If you have taken refuge in a cave and shrugged off the responsibility of your calling, or ignored the wooing of the Spirit, I ask you to steadfastly seek the Lord.

On the run from King Saul, David retreated to his cave. Listen to what came from his heart while he was there:

> *I cry out to the Lord with my voice; with my voice to the Lord I make my supplication. I pour out my complaint before Him; I declare before Him my trouble. When my spirit was overwhelmed within me, then You knew my path. In the way in which I walk they have secretly set a snare for me. Look on my right hand and see, for there is no one who acknowledges me; refuge has failed me; no one cares for my soul. I cried out to You, O Lord: I said, "You are my refuge, my portion in the land of the living. Attend to my cry, for I am brought very low; deliver me from my persecutors, for they are stronger than I. Bring my soul out of prison, that I may praise Your name; the righteous shall surround me, for You shall deal bountifully with me"* (Psalm 142:1-7 NKJV).

Was this the cry of a desperate man, persecuted and broken? Absolutely. David was hiding in the cave because King Saul was trying to kill him. Today, prophetic voices do not always stand in unity and agreement with pastors, teachers, evangelists, and apostles. Consequently, the vessel of prophecy is like a single wheel pulling a cart, unbalanced and ineffective in moving forward. Prophetic voices should come together with the other offices to complement and aid one another. They should strive to outdo other members of the Body in love, care, and nurture. Each office should enhance the other offices.

When David came back from battle, the people sang and rejoiced over David's victory. "*And the women answered one another as they played, and said, Saul hath slain his thousands, and David his ten thousands*" (1 Sam. 18:7). Saul felt extremely threatened by David; his jealousy grew until he determined the only way to be rid of his rage was to kill the one causing his fear. David remained innocent and purehearted. Nevertheless, Saul's distress and murderous heart opened a door to the demonic. David's attempts to quiet Saul with music eventually were ineffective. Twice Saul tried to take David's life with a spear. Why? "*And Saul was afraid of David, because the Lord was with him, and was departed from Saul*" (1 Sam. 18:12). Finally, David was forced to flee for his life.

What situation or spirit has caused some prophetic people and prophets to shut down their gift? Some have been falsely judged. Some have intimidated others (or have been intimidated) because of the anointing and competition between gifts which wreaked havoc in their relationships. There are many excuses, but the real root is fear, competition, and disobedience. This opens them to the operation of a distressing spirit. It's foolish to think every prophet will be respected, honored, and welcomed every time. Even Jesus said, "*...A prophet is not without honor, save in his own country, and in his own house. And He did not many mighty works there because of their unbelief*" (Matt. 13:57-58).

David's protection was to keep himself from offense against Saul. He continued to honor and respect Saul, despite Saul's wrath. Not only did David refrain from harming God's anointed one, he also restrained his servants from doing anything to Saul.

How we respond in the cave is critical. Honoring God's anointed office protects us. Restoration of prophets comes after they forgive those who have offended, harmed, or belittled them. The reasons for the offense may be intentional or unintentional—it makes no difference. We are commanded to forgive those who hurt us. In fact, the Word says we are to "judge not lest we be judged" (see Matt. 7:1). False judgments are a snare that can hold two people in one cave. It's time to open the door and come out! It's time to forgive whomever we need to forgive, because our own unforgiveness will hold us in captivity—not any other person.

The call of God's Spirit is, "where the Spirit of the Lord is there is freedom" (see 2 Cor. 3:17). In order to flow in the prophetic at a high level of purity and authority, _we must be under the absolute authority of God's Spirit_ (see my book "Embraced by the Holy Spirit"). Our flesh can tempt us to rebel and become a renegade that hinders the prophetic. Although David had every right to kill and hate Saul, he feared the Lord and honored the anointed office Saul occupied as king. "The fear of the Lord is the beginning of wisdom..." (Proverbs 9:10).

I have been around the fivefold ministry for many years. I've listened to preachers give incorrect teaching, but never take responsibility for their errors. They did not live under the threat of being cast out or banished because they did not discern the Word of God correctly or teach it to the people perfectly. Perhaps this is because they have not carried the responsibility of concluding every sermon with, "Thus saith the Lord." The Spirit of God is grieved that the Body of Christ has so belittled and disrespected the gift of prophesy and the office of prophet. It's interesting to note that we are to test the fruit, but I believe that testing should not be weighted against the prophet. The same criteria should be used to test all offices.

There should be schools of prophets all around the world to help recognize, raise up, and send out those God has called and appointed. Some of my pastor friends say, "We do not allow prophecy...in fact, we shut it down because not all prophesy is one hundred percent right."

I jokingly reply, "Have all of your sermons been one hundred percent on the mark? If not, we had better clear out the pulpits!" (Give grace to get grace!)

Now this is not a "love walk" issue. If you've read this far in the book, you know I have driven the point home about every gift operating in love. It's a sad day when weak, little people start thinking so highly of themselves that we shoot and kill the "jackass" that was sent to prophesy.

And the Lord opened the mouth of the ass, and she said unto Balaam, What have I done unto thee, that thou hast smitten me these three times? And Balaam said unto the ass, Because thou hast *mocked me: I would there were a sword in mine hand, for now would I kill thee. And the ass said unto Balaam, Am not I thine ass, upon which thou hast ridden ever since I was thine unto this day? Was I ever wont to do so unto thee?* (Numbers 22:28-30)

Our responsibility is to spread the Good News with signs and wonders to a lost world, and to edify, encourage, and strengthen the Body. I have been in healing services where mighty people of God moved in this gift and flowed strong in the anointing. They loved and touched people's lives. Yet, they were not shut down or told to be quiet because 100 percent of the people were not healed! The power of God should be under the rule and reign of the Holy Spirit through imperfect human vessels. It is presumptuous and absurd to think human vessels would place their will above and their ways before God's Spirit.

If you are one who feels whipped and beaten and left to die in your cave alone, there is good news for you! God is saying, "Let go of the past, so the past can let go of you." You can be totally free and at liberty to continue the race you were once running. You may come out crawling and bleeding or strong and secure—this is unimportant. The important part is that you enter back into the operation of your prophetic gifting with humility, love, and the fear of the Lord. Understand that God not only loves you, but loves all of His people.

How Do I Come Back?

How do you reenter the race? If you have allowed people to declare who you are, rather than accepting what God says about you, repent. Perhaps the outcome for King Saul would have been different had he repented for his offenses against David. If Saul were here today and we could ask him, "Was it worth the price to hold onto your jealousy and anger toward David?" I'm not so sure he would say yes. He had no idea what price he would pay for carrying this hatred toward David. Picture Saul lying in bed stressed out because of his own wrong choices. God knew Saul's will. He also knew his heart motives. God intentionally sent a distressing spirit to Saul.

Now the distressing spirit from the Lord came upon Saul as he sat in his house with his spear in his hand. And David was playing music with his hand. Then Saul sought to pin David to the wall with a spear, but he slipped away from Saul's presence; and he drove the spear into the wall. So David fled and escaped that night (1 Samuel 19:9-10 NKJV).

Repent from all ungodly competition and any wrongful words that have come from your lips that do not come from the Father's heart. Close every door that would allow a distressing spirit to operate in your life. In other words, grow in faith and purification in your prophetic calling. Use your prophetic gift for the Kingdom's sake alone. Begin to value, respect, and treasure everyone in the fivefold ministry. God is looking for hands that will link together with others and hearts that will guard each other. Jesus said, *"By this all will know that you are My disciples, if you have love for one another"* (John 13:35). We should not be competing for the attention or wealth of people, but competing to "out-love" and encourage each other to focus our eyes upon Jesus. He alone is the One who sees and rewards things that are done in secret. He will reward us accordingly. A higher way of bringing the Kingdom to earth is to pull down all "sacred cows" of self-idolatry that cause us to idealize one office above another. We must honor and appreciate every gift of the Spirit and respect every office God has ordained.

Some of you have been wounded and sidetracked. You still need time to heal and be restored. The danger in coming out of the cave prematurely is that your woundedness will come through the gifting, as well as reflect in your prayer life. Some of you are at such a low point in your life, you are in crisis and crying out to God like David did. So, it's important to respond like David, *"Bring my soul out of prison, that I may praise Thy name"* (Ps. 142:7a). All the gifts, including prophecy, are meant to serve the Body of Christ. Some servants have a contagious disease caused by anger, grief, sorrow, etc. You do not want to contaminate others as a result of leaving the cave before you've repented or are fully healed. I'm not suggesting a time frame, but what I'm saying is that you should stay in the cave under God's protection and comfort until you are fully healed and restored.

I remember a cave time in my life when I needed healing and laid down the gift of prophecy. I was afraid to use it because I was fearful I'd hurt someone out of my own wounding. Some judged me, saying I was not walking in faith and I was limiting God. They used the Scripture about God's "strength being made perfect in weakness" (see 2 Cor. 12:9). In my heart of hearts I knew that the kindest and most loving thing I could do for the Body was not to prophesy at that time. It was a time of pain, confusion, anger, and testing of my faith.

Thirteen years ago, our only son, Michael, died from a heart attack at age 26. My severe shock and terror prompted me to shut down my ministry for one year. Some encouraged me to take two weeks off and jump back into the ministry. However, I knew I was not healed or ready by the way I responded to phone calls and speaking invitations.

Two weeks after my son's funeral, I received a call from a minister at a woman's prison. She asked me to pray, prophesy, and teach these women. I shocked myself by my response to her: "You don't want me to come and tell the women what I think about God right now." I hung up on her. I'm very sorry that happened, and I later asked her forgiveness. That incident was a red flag to me. Prophecy is both about loving and caring for others and about being the one who is privileged to hear God's precious, awesome voice.

Some of you need to be honest, forthright, and realistic about your thoughts and feelings toward God. Your words are a mirror that can be held up to your soul—they can be words of peace, hope, and healing or of anger, fear, and frustration. God longs to restore the souls of His own. God is still in the business of bringing souls out of prison so we can praise Him. The person you are praying for is the most important person at that moment, just as I spoke of earlier in this book. This keeps our motives pure and our love intact toward the Body of Christ.

By God's Spirit and love, I would like to personally escort some of you to the cave and lock you in! I would do it for your safety as well as the safety of others. Whether intentionally or not, you have spoken your own words and not those of the Spirit. You have perhaps hurt pastors, churches, and innocent people. I admonish you to make love your highest aim! Place yourself under a trustworthy, wise advisor or spiritual counselor. Give that person the reins of your gifting to help control your mouth and guard your heart. Do not allow your words to be used as a weapon against God's precious, wonderful people.

You may wonder which category you fall into: ready to leave the cave, remaining in the cave for a season of healing, or being locked in the cave until shown your true calling. I recommend you proceed just like the apostles after Jesus was crucified. They found themselves in an upper room waiting for the confirmation and direction of the Holy Spirit. Such confirmation and direction may come to you through a wise counselor, pastor, brother, or sister in Christ who clearly hear God's voice, care for you, and are willing to invest in your life.

Some of you may be thinking, *That is a great idea, but I have no one like that.* Begin asking God to place you in a group or with an individual who will fill this role for you. In whatever category you find yourself, you have the same heavenly value. We have all been paid for with the same price—His blood. It makes us all equal, but unique—just as all the gifts of the Spirit are different, but of equal value. All positions in the Body are honored and respected. This is the way of God.

WE ARE ALL CALLED

What is the assignment of a prophet? It is the same as the other offices of the fivefold ministry: pastors, teachers, evangelists, apostles, and prophets. They should all have the same goal, vision, and heart to equip the Body of Christ. They must have the mind of Christ and circumspectly apply themselves to the perfecting of the saints, the work of the ministry, and the edifying of the Body of Christ until *"we all come in the unity of the faith, and of the knowledge of the Son of God, unto a perfect man, unto the measure of the stature of the fullness of Christ"* (Eph. 4:13).

Again, we are all called because of the precious and wonderful blood of Jesus. We all have a specific purpose and position in Christ Jesus. Each and every one of us, no matter how small our part in the Body of Christ, is indispensable. We all share the responsibility of ushering in the Kingdom and will of God on the earth. He is looking for those who will allow Him to use their mouth as His mouthpiece, so they will declare with authority and truth that Jesus Christ is Lord.

I fell at his feet to worship him. And he said unto me, "See thou do it not: I am thy fellowservant, and of thy brethren that have the testimony of Jesus: worship God: for **the testimony of Jesus is the spirit of prophecy"** (Revelation 19:10).

Heavenly Father,

I worship You and bow down to You. I praise You for Your love, faithfulness, and wisdom. I thank You, Father, that when You created me You also created a position for me to fill. I thank You that You have equipped me and are placing me strategically in my highest giftings and highest office or position, so that Jesus' name be glorified. Father, thank You that You love me enough to heal me. You also love Your people and are going to use me as an instrument to bring healing to others. Please confirm my purpose, position, and destiny. I ask not to wander or hide in a cave any longer than necessary.

Lay Your hand upon me right now and separate me for such a time as this. Father, my times and seasons are in Your hands. Order my steps and let me hear Your sweet commands. Pour Your favor over me and make me grow in stature and favor with You and man. I give You my agenda. I give You my plans. I ask that, as Jesus took water and turned it into wine during a wedding celebration, You would turn my life into Your good pleasure and prepare me for the King of kings and Lord of lords. I praise You and bless You that Your banner over me is love. Give me the grace, the humility, and the strength to pick up that banner of love and place it over the lives of your precious, wonderful people. Father, use me for Your glory.

In the wonderful name of Your Son Jesus, Amen.

Devotional

Key Scriptures: Psalm 142:1-7; 1 Samuel 18:7; 1 Samuel 18:12; Matthew 13:57-58; Numbers 22:28-30; 1 Samuel 19:9-10; John 13:35; Ephesians 4:13; Revelation 19:10.

Key Point: Prophetic voices are those called to be the heralds of good news.

CALLING ALL PROPHETS

1. Many people who at one time were prophesying and called to occupy the office of a prophet:
   a. Became offended
   b. Became wounded
   c. Were discouraged through weariness
   d. All of the above

2. "Today prophetic voices do not always _____ and _____ with pastors, teachers, evangelists, and apostles. Consequently, the vessel of prophecy is like a single wheel pulling a cart, _____ and _____ in moving forward."

3. "Restoration of prophets comes after they forgive those who have offended, harmed, or belittled them." True of False?

4. Are all sermons 100 percent perfect? Yes, No, or Maybe. (Circle one.)

5. "It is _____ and _____ to think human vessels would place their will above and their ways before God's Spirit."

How Do I Come Back?

6. How do you reenter the prophetic arena?

_____

_____

_____

7. "A higher way of bringing the Kingdom to earth is to pull down all _____ of _____ that cause us to idealize one office above another."

8. "Prophecy is both about loving and caring for others and about being the one who is privileged to hear God's precious, awesome voice." True of False?

9. I would admonish you to:
    a. Love others
    b. Seek power
    c. Desire ambition
    d. Compete with others

We Are All Called

10. Are we all called? Yes or No. Why?

_____

_____

_____

11. What are you called to do to usher in the Kingdom of God on the earth? Are you actively pursuing this call?

_____

_____

_____

12. We all share the responsibility of _____ and _____.

13. Remember, "*The* _____ *of Jesus is the* _____ *of* _____" (Revelation 19:10).

Devotional Answer Key

Chapter 1: The Calling

1. f
2. Love, support, agreement, safe setting, feeling free to grow
3. Authority
4. Stronger and stronger
5. Prophecies
6. True

Chapter 2: Prophets of Old

1. Joel
2. Certain time, certain place, certain message, certain group of people
3. e
4. False
5. 'This is what the Lord says.'

Chapter 3: Who's Speaking Now?

1. Life, death
2. Edify, encourage, and strengthen
3. God

4. *Spirit, spirits, prophets*
5. a and b
6. Soulish motives
7. false
8. [Prophets of the land] are usually ambitious for land, power, or position. Prophets of the Lord prophesy His word and stand against other voices of strange prophets.
9. False prophets
10. Stay in submission; voice; will of God.
11. Worthless; vision; heart; the mouth of the Lord

Chapter 4: "In the Hot Seat"

1. False
2. Submission
3. "I want you to stand up, pray truth, and speak a word that will set her free."

4. Personal answer and group discussion.

Chapter 5: The Counterfeit Versus the Genuine

1. "...I saw your aura, it was a bright green, and your energy field was full of great energy, representing healing."

2. New Age

3. g

4. False

5. Psychics; prophets; instruments in the hand of a loving God.

6. a

7. "if"

8. The arm of the Lord

9. He had forsaken God and was living in wicked, rebellious ways.

Chapter 6: The Showdown

1. People recognize Him as the Lord

2. Witchcraft

3. Return to the written Word of God and the Holy Spirit's discernment.

4. How to stay humble

5. The gifts of the Holy Spirit, including the gift of discernment of spirits.

6. c

7. Yes

8. "I" (all three blanks)

9. A soulish word (Personal answer and group discussion.)

Chapter 7: Prophetic Interference

1. The fear of the Lord

2. You; Me

3. Because death cannot respond to or acknowledge the beckoning of the Holy Spirit.

4. Laughing; with rejoicing

5. c (actually e—this is a yoke question)

Chapter 8: Integrity of the Prophetic

1. Angry; unteachable; offended; standing behind the word of the Lord

2. True

3. It becomes a declarative voice of the Lord through His prophets to catch a glimpse of God's eternal plan that is still continuing to unfold upon the earth.

4. True; *"Surely the Lord does nothing, unless He reveals His secret to His servants the prophets"* (Amos 3:7).

5. An unholy agreement, an ungodly alliance

6. Always

7. Free will; agreement; build his rebellious kingdom

8. The one who carries the anointing.

Chapter 9: How to Hear

1. Unction

2. This is the unction of the Holy Spirit drawing from your spirit. This is the Lord's way of letting you know He wants to make a withdrawal from your "bucket" to build up the Body of Christ.

3. Rivers of living water

4. A prompting, tugging or very strong impression from the Holy Spirit

5. Bee is drawn; honey

6. Fervent love; love; multitude

7. b and e

Chapter 10: Prophetic Humility

1. Go back in the Spirit and listen to what the Holy Spirit is speaking. (Personal answer and group discussion.)

2. Cheshire cat; cheese

3. Shut down the prophetic (although satan does all three)

Chapter 11: Becoming His Mouthpiece

1. True

2. To stay in His presence, face to face, in order to clearly hear His voice

3. Yes; John 4:19

4. *Call your husband; no husband; had five husbands; one you have now is not your husband*

5. *Grace; prophecy; prophesy; faith*

6. c

7. True

8. John the Baptist leaped in her womb (Luke 1:41).

9. Drown out the counterfeit sounds of the psychics; wolves in sheep's clothing; all voices trying to rise above the voice of the Spirit of God.

10. Love and care more for God's treasured people

11. Intercede; stand in the gap

12. Yes

13. e

Chapter 12: Passing the Grade

1. False (If you said true, please re-read the "Sweet Lisa" story.)

2. a. Seal of the Holy Spirit
   b. Approval of the Holy Spirit
   c. Fear of the Lord
   d. Wisdom

Chapter 13: A Time and Place

1. Personal answer and group discussion.

2. Limited; where; when

Chapter 14: Warring With the Prophetic

1. Wage the good warfare (1 Timothy 1:18)

2. True

3. *Warfare* is "a military operation between enemies," and an activity undertaken by one country (or kingdom) to weaken or destroy another. The application is that satan is trying to overthrow God's Kingdom and halt our part in God's army to establish His will on the earth.

4. *logos*—written; *rhema*—enlightenment, leaps out, becomes alive, illuminated

5. No—Even the devil knows the Word of God, so why would you consider letting him use God's sword on you? (Personal answer and group discussion.)

6. He was making sure satan knew He (Jesus) was God.

7. By pulling up our own "spiritual bootstraps" and vigorously running the race of faith.
8. d
9. Losing battle; won war

Chapter 15: Winning the War

1. e
2. He only watches over His words to perform them.
3. "over and above; to conquer describes one who is super victorious and wins more than an ordinary victory, but who is overpowering in achieving abundant victory" (*Strong's Concordance*)
4. Yes (2 Timothy 4:7)
5. Conscience without offense
6. An examination of our own conscience
7. Conversations discussing others' weaknesses and sin; gossip, slander, etc.
8. False
9. Agreement
10. Pride; root of bitterness; unresolved anger; unforgiveness; disobedience
11. After we yield to sin over and over again, the enemy's foothold becomes stronger and stronger and establishes a stronghold.
12. We do

Chapter 16: Survivors and Casualties of War

1. g
2. Ambition; pride; My Spirit
3. Life-giving words full of hope

4. True
5. "*For God is not the author of confusion but of peace...*" (1 Corinthians 14:33).

Chapter 17: Prophetic Visions and Dreams

1. "something seen otherwise than by ordinary sight as in a dream or a trance" (*Webster's Dictionary*)
2. Yes—Some of God's prophecies and promises are conditional
3. Free will
4. Yes
5. Jesus
6. Perfect will (He was conceived, born, ordained, crucified, and resurrected in God's perfect will.)
7. Natural
8. e
9. Many times with open visions it is as if a neon light or picture is hung out in midair for us to view.
10. False (1 Corinthians 2:14-16)
11. True
12. He saw a vision (Acts 10:10).
13. d
14. Prayed and fasted
15. Run with a vision; write down a vision
16. Yes—"*For the vision is yet for an appointed time, but at the end it shall speak and not lie*" (Habakkuk 2:3).
17. True—"*For though it tarry, wait for it, because it will surely come, it will not tarry*" (Habakkuk 2:3).
18. e
19. True

20. No—remember, Jesus prophesied over the woman at the well.

Chapter 18: Where Are the Prophets?

1. d
2. Stand in unity, agreement; unbalanced, ineffective
3. True
4. No
5. Presumptuous; absurd
6. Repent if you have allowed people to declare who you are, rather than accepting what God says about you.
7. "Sacred cows"; self-idolatry
8. True
9. a
10. Yes; because of the precious and wonderful blood of Jesus
11. Personal answer and discussion.
12. Ushering in the Kingdom; will of God on earth
13. Testimony; Spirit; prophecy

AUTHORS CONTACT PAGE

EILEEN FISHER MINISTRIES INC.
P.O. BOX 26211
COLORADO SPRINGS, CO 80936-6211
(719) 272-7091

E-mail eileen@eileenfisher.org

Website www.eileenfisher.org

Additional copies of this book and other
book titles from DESTINY IMAGE are
available at your local bookstore.

Call toll free: 1-800-722-6774.

Send a request for a catalog to:

Destiny Image® Publishers, Inc.

P.O. Box 310
Shippensburg, PA 17257-0310

*"Speaking to the Purposes of God for this
Generation and for the Generations to Come."*

**For a complete list of our titles,
visit us at www.destinyimage.com**